FROM W
TO [

Austin Bidwell

FROM WALL STREET TO NEWGATE

Austin Bidwell

TRUE
CRIME
LIBRARY

True Crime Library
A Forum Press Book
by the Paperback Division of
Forum Design,
P.O. Box 158, London SE20 7QA

An Imprint of True Crime Library
© 1996 Mike James
All rights reserved

Typeset by T D Studio
16-18 Paxton Place, Hamilton Road,
Gypsy Hill SE27 9SS
Printed and bound in Great Britain by
Caledonian, Bishopbriggs, Glasgow
ISBN 1 874358 12 5

Austin Bidwell

"Austin, I've found you a job on Wall Street" (Chapter 1)

Newgate Prison where the conspirators were held

CONTENTS

FOREWORD

If there is somewhere a Valhalla of celebrity fraudsters, Austin Byron Bidwell must rank with the greatest of them all – alongside Horatio Bottomley, Ivan Kreuger, Robert Maxwell and others of their ilk.

As young confidence tricksters who took on the late nineteenth century financial world, Bidwell and his accomplices – notably the coldly calculating George Macdonnell – have no equals. The cavalier way in which they roamed the world in the guise of rich men, tricking what at that time were huge sums of money out of banks and finance houses before they moved in for their big killing on the Bank of England, was original and ingenious, besides being fraught with risks and dangers.

Shortly before his death Austin Bidwell wrote an account of his life, embracing his extraordinary near-£1 million fraud on the Bank of England, his amazing career of fraud before the Bank job, and his incredible adventures after it. His narrative was unstructured, sometimes contradictory, and frequently moralising. This book is an attempt to sort out the discrepancies, and reduce the embellishment without detracting from Bidwell's style.

First-person narratives seldom give descriptions of the main players, whose physical attributes the author knows so well that he may not stop to think that his readers might like to know too. This was the case with Bidwell's narrative. We are left wondering what sort of men were these, apart from being larger than life and supremely confident in themselves? What did they actually look like?

The few sketchy accounts of the Bank of England fraud, apart, from Austin Bidwell's, are hostile to the conspirators. They are couched in terms that the Bank of England luminaries of the 1870s would have approved of: Bidwell was a scoundrel, a ruffian, a Yankee rogue and all sorts of other things which give no clues to the actual man. The nearest we get to him is in the police description of the wanted "F. A. Warren", who was Austin Bidwell. He was "very thin and bony, between 30 and 35" (he was in fact still in his twenties), "but looking older, with black, wavy hair, dark whiskers and moustache."

George Macdonnell was "strongly built, of gentlemanly appearance, around 30 years old, about 5 ft. 10 ins., fair complexion, dark brown hair, inclined to baldness, with a high forehead and small blue eyes. He speaks several Continental languages".

Austin's eldest brother George was described as "a man of middle height, nearing 40, sallow complexion, black hair, and beard and whiskers, recently shaved off, rather strongly built and generally carrying a black bag".

Both "Warren" and Macdonnell were described as usually wearing large diamond rings.

Macdonnell was said by the Victorian English press to have "a shady reputation" in America, and probably the quarrel with his father, which Austin Bidwell refers to, arose out of some nefarious dealings in the United States.

In Europe Austin Bidwell used six aliases, George Bidwell 16, Macdonnell 13 and Edwin Noyes, in his short stay in Britain, ran up a total of six.

In his narrative Bidwell made passing reference to a

Newgate warder who received a bribe from a prisoner and as a result was imprisoned for 18 months. That reference has been omitted from this book, but it is interesting to know what actually happened – the part Bidwell himself left out.

While the four conspirators were being held at Newgate, John Bidwell, a brother of Austin and George, came over from America and offered three Newgate warders £100 each if they would help him effect an escape plan. The idea was that the four prisoners should be helped to escape from their cells at night.

If it succeeded John Bidwell would add an additional £1,000 to the senior warder's fee.

The warders accepted the bribe, but the plot leaked out after the senior warder made the mistake of telling a detective friend that he was planning to emigrate to Tasmania with money he was going to receive from the brother of two of the prisoners.

The three warders were suspended. The senior warder was brought before a magistrate at the Guildhall and sent to prison for 18 months. It is this man to whom Austin Bidwell fleetingly referred, without saying why he was bribed or who bribed him.

Even after that John Bidwell managed to stay in touch with the prisoners and hatch a second escape plan involving the four leaping from the dock during the preliminary hearing at the Lord Mayor of London's court. This plot, too, was discovered, and an alderman on the bench ordered that all the court doors leading to the street should be locked and guarded throughout the hearing. All the warders were removed from the court and their places were taken by six armed policemen.

Where Bidwell's account of his activities can be checked against newspaper reports during 1872 and 1863, his narrative is completely accurate.

Perhaps understandably, however, he confesses to being reluctant to dwell upon his Old Bailey trial, and dismisses it scornfully in a few sentences. In the belief that his story is incomplete without it, an account of the trial is included as an appendix.

For readers not conversant with the complexities of the nineteenth century financial world, Bidwell is an excellent tutor, but it is worth remembering that at the time of these events one pound sterling was valued at between four and four and a half dollars. And for a rough guide to the progress in value of the pound during the last 100 years, multiply all the sterling figures in this book by 100 – that is, add two noughts to Austin Bidwell's figures – and you get some idea in present-day terms of the enormity of his fraudulent operations.

1

A CITY OF CROOKED COPS

Standing at the intersection of a whole bunch of streets opposite the Bank of England and viewing that impressive institution for the very first time in my life, I said to my two companions: "That's the one we should bust. It could be the biggest one of all time. Hit it for a million pounds and we'll be made for life."

We were three young Americans on holiday doing Europe. That morning we'd strolled round Hampton Court, returning to London by boat on the Thames to lunch at the Cannon Street Hotel. We were taking an afternoon stroll through the City, watching the human whirlpool in that centre of throbbing life, when I espied the famous Old Lady of Threadneedle Street.

My companions made no reply to my instinctive remark. But next day we took a trip to see Windsor Castle. It was in the throne room there that Mac – George MacDonnell, the intellectual of our trio – said:

"Something you mentioned yesterday's been nagging at me ever since. We need a hundred thousand pounds each to make this trip worthwhile before we head for home. That Bank of England's got plenty of cash to spare. I bet it's really fossilised, up to its neck in dry rot, I'd guess. It shouldn't be that difficult."

"The Brits have a saying 'Safe as the Bank of England,'" my brother George, who made up our party, chipped in. He had his back to us and was studying a case of decorations. Then he added: "You could be right, though. All the big nobs in institutions like that get their jobs through the old boy network. They think they're impregnable, which is exactly why they're vulnerable, of course."

So there we were, three Yanks still in our twenties, leaning up against the wall of the throne room of Windsor Castle, discussing how we were going to knock a million out of the Bank of England. And like all good ideas, once that one got stuck between our ears, it just wouldn't budge.

That night we sat over dinner in the twilight of an old inn a stone's throw from Threadneedle Street and talked it through.

"A pompous label like 'the Governor and Company of the Bank of England' has just got to mask a bunch of dummies," George said.

"The whole place will crumble under a bold frontal attack," declared Mac.

Yankee bravado, you're thinking? You're wrong. We were serious, deadly serious. When I look back on it I wish to hell we hadn't been half so serious. But as I said, the idea was planted firmly between three sets of ears, and it was growing three sets of roots.

In fact, the plan we worked on far into that night had every chance of success. We knew it would create an international furore once we'd made off with the cash. Curiously, we didn't give much thought to that. We were young, and we knew we had the experience, the skill and the verve needed to pull it off. Let me tell you why we planned to strike where angels feared to tread ...

I was 16, fresh out of school, and we were living in South Brooklyn when my father came back from New York one day and said gravely: "Austin, I've found you a job on Wall Street."

It sounded good. It was in the office of a sugar broker called Waterbury. When I turned up for duty the following week I was introduced to two other employees there who were to have some influence on my learning curve. One was Waterbury's amiable clerk, Mr. Ambler, who was to teach me about finance. The other was a junior like me named Harry, who knew his way around and fired my imagination with stories of speculators making fortunes in the gold-room or on the Exchange.

Mr. Ambler didn't take long to see what a bad influence Harry was having on me. So when he resigned after a year for health reasons, he showed sufficient interest in my welfare to get me a job with a firm of brokers in New Street.

I was to get ten bucks a week, which was interesting cash in those days. It allowed me to dress the part; more importantly it brought me in touch with some of the very folks on Wall Street from whom kind Mr. Ambler had tried to protect me. One, a real sharpie, was Ed Weed. He worked on his own account and used to come regularly to our broker's office. He seemed to take a shine for me, and pretty soon we were real buddies.

"You're not really dressed for the job, kid," Ed confided to me one day. "Come along and meet my tailor. He'll soon have you looking right."

We walked uptown together after close of business and, prompted by Ed, I ordered $150 worth of suits. Immediately afterwards he took me to his outfitter, where I spent as much again on shirts, shoes and other stuff. No one seemed to mind that I didn't have more than five bucks in my pocket. It all went straight on the slate.

I expect you're thinking, ah, here's trouble, Ed is leading him straight down the slippery path into debt. Well, you're wrong. My employers were so knocked out by my sartorial splendour that they raised my salary to $30 a week. Then, piloted by Ed, I ventured $50 on a margin on gold and won. I invested again and again, and in a fortnight I was $284 ahead. I paid my tailor and my outfitter's bill, bought a $100 watch on credit, and gave a wine supper on borrowed cash. A few weeks later Ed and I started out on our own, trading as E. Weed and Co.

We were in the back end of the 1860s, when all stocks were on the boom. America was speculation-crazy, you could smell the bucks all down Wall Street. We got plenty of commissions, made tons of dough. The problem was we went through it as fast as we made it. We gambled on shares during the day, and at night we gambled in the casinos. The problem got bigger when we started losing more by night than we were making by day.

In the end we were saved only by Ed's wealthy parents. They bailed us out for a tidy sum, and although that stopped me frequenting the gambling joints, it didn't stop my extravagant life-style, wining and dining and being dined and wined. It was this propensity for good living which really started me on the up and up – or the down and down, whichever way you look at it.

One cold January night I was dining with several friends in a Fifth Avenue hotel when the restaurant door swung open and a flush-faced, heavily set fellow strode in.

"Well, look who's here," breathed Tony, one of my party. "It's Jimmy Irving, the biggest crook in New York."

"Jimmy," called out my pal Sidney. "Come over and join us."

You can imagine my rather more than slight surprise in view of Tony's label for him, when Jimmy Irving came over and was introduced to me as Captain Irving, Chief of the New York Detective Force.

Jimmy sat down next to me, ordered a T-bone and fries, and soon discovered that with the row going on all around us it was easier to talk to me than across the table. I reckon I'm pretty smart at weighing up bums, and I was soon reckoning that Captain Irving was just about the biggest bum I'd ever met. It was clear that he was where he was only because the New York Police Department was rotten with corruption and this maggot at its core was a bit more greedy than the rest of them. For all that I liked talking to him, and more importantly, he seemed to like me. During the time he ate his steak and fries he ordered three bottles of expensive wine for our table, and polished off one of them himself. He said he would have liked to have stayed, but he had to get back to 300 Mulberry Street, Police Headquarters. Still, it was really nice knowing you, Austin, and before he shook hands all round he and I had arranged to meet socially the following Sunday.

After Jimmy had gone I asked Tony about him.

"He gets his biggest rake-off from the Tenderloin," Tony said. The Tenderloin was the New York police precinct, from Spring Street to Tenth, crossed by Broadway, an area which was then home to about half the city's whores and a dozen gambling joints. "It pays him probably around a thousand bucks a week. There's around five other big-shot cops in the ring with him, but he gets the most."

"He said he'd like to see if he could do some business with me."

Tony and the others went quiet. Then Tony said: "He could put you in the way of big bucks, Austin. But you may have to decide if that's the kind of cash you want to make."

I shrugged and changed the conversation. I soon forgot all about Captain Jimmy Irving, until next Sunday, when there was a ring at my doorbell.

Jimmy had a rig outside with a fast trotting horse, that must have cost him a thousand dollars. He was also sporting a diamond tie-pin that was eye-boggling, and I reckon that as his legitimate city-paid earnings were around two thousand a year, the rig and pin had cost him a year's salary.

"Let's drive up to Westchester County," he suggested. As we headed north, I knew I was being scrutinised, like a guy being given the once-over for a big high-powered job. But Jimmy never let on. He doffed his hat to all manner of people as we drove uptown, and reeled off a string of amusing anecdotes about the Police

Department. At Westchester we had a sumptuous lunch at O'Brien's Hotel, which Jimmy insisted on paying for. After lunch the sun got warm for a couple of hours, and we drove back with big cigars on and at peace with the world.

"Like to look in on headquarters?" Jimmy asked. "Some of my best lads are on duty just now."

I could scarcely say no, because it was being telegraphed to me that I had passed muster and was now about to be given the once-over by two more crooked cops. But if you ask me didn't I think it was all a bit fishy, the answer is no. Jimmy bought the very best wine and the very best cigars, and being susceptible to both, I was more intent on enjoying them than asking what they were for. So we went into the headquarters building, and there were Chief Detective Stanley and Chief Detective White, shaking hands with me warmly and looking every bit like two guys you wanted to keep on the right side of.

Twenty-four hours later I had all but forgotten them. For Ed came into the office next day looking terrible, and anyone could see he was ill. I soon found out what probably caused it. He'd thrown a lot of his papa's cash at a stock which had come unstuck, and we were in big crisis again. This time we couldn't expect to be bailed out. The following week Ed announced he was quitting.

"I'm going to Europe, to Italy for my health," he said. "There's nothing in the office to share out except for the furniture, and you can have that."

I went down to the port and saw him off several days later. He was travelling with a couple of members of his family, and he looked pretty ghastly. The truth was he'd been leading a dissolute life and it showed. I should have learned a lesson from him there and then, for I never saw him again, and he never came back to America. Twelve months later his father told me Ed had died in Italy.

I was twenty years old, on my own, and feeling very

lonesome. One evening I was coming out of Wallack's Theatre when who should I run into but Captain Jimmy Irving. We shook hands warmly.

"Come and have a spot of dinner," he said. Delmonico's was just round the corner, and again he insisted on paying for everything. After another grand feast we walked round to the St. Denis Hotel at Broadway and Eleventh and who should we find there but Chief Detective Stanley and Chief Detective White. A couple of bottles of French wine later I found myself actually liking these guys. It never occurred to me then that when you're lonely in New York City you can like just about anyone who talks to you. Well, we talked, or rather, I did most of it, about stocks and shares and bulls and bears and the fine art of brokering, and all over lots more wine. I remember looking up at the clock and thinking, my God, it's gone two, and the room had long since emptied, when Irving suddenly leaned forward, tapped me confidentially on the knee of my very expensive suit and said: "You know, kid, you're all right. A pretty sound businessman for your age, I reckon. We'd like to do some business with you, 'cause we think we could all make ourselves a lot of dough."

White passed his cigar case under my nose, and Jimmy went on: "Why don't we all have dinner tomorrow night at Delmonico's and see if we can come up with a nice proposition."

"I'd really like that, Jimmy," I said warmly.

So the next evening I was getting myself togged up when there was a ring at the doorbell. It was White.

"Change of venue, Austin," he said. "The Chief doesn't want to go to Delmonico's." He named another restaurant at Sixth Avenue and 31st Street, and when I got there an hour later I realised why he had changed – the new restaurant had a private room.

A waiter was hanging about on the doorstep, evidently on the look-out for me, and as soon as he reckoned he'd got the right man he ushered me upstairs to a private room. Another waiter was standing at the door like a guardsman on sentry duty. White was already inside, having a drink, and soon afterwards Irving and Stanley came in together. We started with champagne and an amuse-gueule; then came smoked salmon, followed by soup, then tête de veau. I was just working out what percentage of Jimmy Irving's police salary would be left after he'd paid for this lot when once again he leaned forward confidentially and said with oily candour:

"How would you like to do us a small favour and make ten grand for yourself?"

Ten grand! My eyes popped. I hadn't been within light years of that kind of cash since Ed took off.

"How?" was all I could say.

"We'd like to give you some bonds and send you to Europe to negotiate them for us." He paused. "They're stolen, of course, but that shouldn't give a smart chap like you any trouble."

"And you'll have the protection of the New York Police Department behind you," smiled Stanley.

"I've never been on the crook," I said dubiously.

"Well, think about it, kid," Irving said. "You don't have to give your answer straightaway. Come and see us in a day or two if you like. This could be a nice job and some easy money for you."

I didn't sleep much that night, and I was bug-eyed with tiredness next morning when there was a knock at the office door. It was the landlord's agent, a little ferret of a fellow with a blond moustache, and a weak mouth and chin.

"I'm afraid we can't allow these rent arrears to keep on slipping," he said smoothly. "We shall need a cheque for $500 within thirty days, and a separate cheque for sundry services supplied, which you will find listed here."

He handed me a note. He might just as well have handed me a ticket for Europe.

A hell of a lot of people don't know much about big-city finance, so those who do are going to have to forgive me for a moment while I do some explaining. Before 1861 white-collar crime was hardly known in the States. The reason was that the country's currency was strictly limited. There were no government bonds or currency, and the few bonds issued by corporations were not usually made payable to bearer, and therefore not being negotiable were useless to thieves. But in 1861, to meet the anticipated Civil War expenses, the State banks were taxed out of existence and the national currency system came into being.

Besides the enormous issue of greenbacks, bonds payable to bearer amounting to hundreds of millions were issued by the Government, and by individual states, counties, towns and cities, and all became popular investments. Patriotism, and of course profit, led banks, corporations and individuals all over the world to invest surplus funds in bonds, and the most popular were those issued by the Government. The various issues authorised by act of Congress were known as "seven-thirties", "ten-forties", "five-twenties", etc., terms denoting the rate of interest (first figure) and the period of years, dating from the first issue, in which it was optional for the Government to redeem them. So in a few short years the buzz phrases around town were "seven-thirties" and "ten-forties", and since most people were speculating, most people knew what they meant. The business of the express companies of the United States boomed as for the first time in their history they began to be the carriers of vast sums from city to city.

For thieves just as much as speculators this was a good time to live. Only nuts now burglarised bank safes for the gold in them; what the smart burglar looked for was bearer bonds. Let me give you an example. In mid-century there was a very wealthy property developer named George Lord who had inherited millions. Lord had an office in Broad Street, from where he managed his estates. The office was quiet and had few visitors, because no business was transacted in it except for that which concerned the estates. Lord had invested \$1.2 million in seven-thirties and lulled into a false sense of security by the nature of his rather exclusive workplace, he kept the bearer bonds in his old-fashioned office safe. I know that seems plumb crazy today, with safe-deposit boxes everywhere, but in the middle of the last century it didn't seem so daft. One million two hundred thousand dollars in gold would weigh upwards of a ton, and would be difficult to handle, but the same sum in bonds hardly filled a carpet bag.

The gang that got Lord's bonds was what in police and thieves' slang was known as on the office, because they went around visiting offices in business parts of the city. It consisted of three men, Hod Ennis, Charley Rose, and a man by the name of Bullard. One day they called on Lord's office when he wasn't there; the place was in the charge of two guys who had grown grey in the service of the Lord estate. The bonds were kept in a tin box slightly larger than a soap box and because the interest on them was due, the box had been taken out so that the coupons could be cut off, and left in the open door of the safe. Curiously, none of these circumstances were known to Ennis, Rose and Bullard. They were merely out looking for chances and stumbled on this cracker.

The method they used was the tried and trusted method of on the office gangs. Rose went in first and made some spurious inquiry about the whereabouts of a firm which he knew was a block away down the street. This occupied the attention of one of the two clerks, who took him to a window to show him which way to go. While this was happening Bullard went in, leaving the office door open behind him, and began to chat up the other clerk about some letter he produced from his pocket. Then Ennis arrived, went to the safe, casually picked up the tin box and made off with it, seen only by his two companions. They found a quick pretext to quit

the office without arousing the suspicions of either of the
two clerks, who as a matter of fact did not miss the box
for nearly an hour.

Ennis carried the box to a local tavern, closely followed by his two pals, and when they opened it they
were stunned to find it packed full of bonds all payable
to bearer. Ennis and Rose had no idea what to do with
them, but Bullard was no fool, and realising that it was
important to get some cash before the thing was noised
around, he started out to sell some, agreeing to meet
Rose and Ennis some time later at another tavern.

Bullard went to different brokers' officers and disposed
of ten bonds for $5,000 and stopped at that. He split the
cash with Ennis and Rose, and all three hit the town. By
the next morning they had spent, loaned or gambled
every cent of the $5,000.

News of the Lord heist took Wall Street by storm, but
the weird thing about it was that no complaint was ever
made to the police. When he was interviewed by police
and reporters Lord wouldn't even admit he'd been
robbed, and said if he had been he would prefer to lose
the money rather than have a fuss made.

The biggest frenzy of excitement was inevitably at
300 Mulberry Street, Police Headquarters. Before midnight on the day of the robbery every cop and every
crook in town knew that Hod Ennis and Co. had hit the
big time. Everyone guessed it was from the Lord coup,
but there wasn't a scrap of evidence to finger them.
Meanwhile the gang were proving they were much better thieves than businessmen. Within the next few days
$100,000 of bonds was completely dissipated. Some
were sold to buyers of stolen goods for a percentage of
their value, some were lost in gambling joints, mostly at
Morrissey's, or at Mike Murray's on Broadway, near
Spring Street, and probably some went in the direction
of Mulberry Street. Despite the pay-offs, the net was
closing in, and fearing arrest Ennis fled to Canada,
Bullard to Europe and Rose to California. Eventually

Ennis was convicted of a crime committed some time before. He was sentenced to a hefty stretch, and came out an old, busted guy, penniless and friendless. Rose got five years for another crime, then disappeared. Bullard settled down in Paris. He later returned to the States and planned the huge Boylston Bank robbery in Boston. With his share of the loot he went back to Paris and opened an American bar at the Grand Hotel. After a few years he was short of cash, did a robbery in Belgium, got caught and was put away for life.

If I'm giving you the impression that the whole of New York was crooked in the roaring Sixties and Seventies, I've just about got it right. And now I was about to quit being the odd man out. I had called in on Irving at his office and a look of immense relief passed over his face, and the podgy faces of Stanley and White when I told them I would take their stolen bonds to Europe and negotiate them there. Irving slapped me on the back delightedly.

"I knew you were a good kid from the moment I saw you," he confided. "You were the only man I'd have trusted." He thought for a moment. "Of course, the only security you can give us is your word, but that's all we need, you understand."

"How did you get hold of the bonds?" I said. I thought as I was now the most important member of the gang I was entitled to know.

The three of them began to weave a web of amazing lies, tripping each other up, contradicting each other's stories, so that it was a laugh just listening to them and nodding my head. I learned afterwards that the bonds were a part of the Lord haul.

"Well, I said. "I'll need some cash to pay for my expenses."

I could see at once they hadn't thought of that. Their faces fell.

"No problem," I said. "Give me a thousand-dollar bond and I'll borrow a thousand from a buddy, using the bond as security. My pal won't inspect the bond number, and I'll pay the thousand when I get back and receive the bond again."

Irving slowly opened a drawer in his desk and took out a bond. Without even looking at it, I walked out, saying, "I'll be back in ten minutes." Like all crooks, he was suspicious of everyone – I could see the fear in his eyes as I went out through the door. In his ignorance of Wall Street he probably thought it would at least be a difficult and lengthy business to raise $1,000 on a bond, so I grinned at his undisguised surprise when I came back ten minutes later with ten one-hundreds in my hand. That made a big impression on Jimmy Irving and I wasn't surprised when he handed over the rest of the bonds and told me I had his entire confidence.

But I didn't want to take too much of that sort of crap so I truncated the rest of the conversation by announcing that I'd go to Europe at once. That afternoon I bought a ticket for the Cunard liner *Russia*; two days later I was sailing out of New York harbour bound for Liverpool.

If you're wondering why we thought it was necessary to put 3,000 miles between the theft and the sale of the bonds, let me tell you why. First, bonds issued by the American Government and held in Europe, chiefly in Holland and Germany, were so enormous in volume and passed so freely from hand to hand, that it was easy for a well-dressed, well-spoken guy to sell any quantity even if they were stolen, for the law held that the innocent holder couldn't be deprived of them. Secondly, one great advantage a dishonest man had in Europe at that time – especially an American – was that if he was well dressed he was considered a gentleman, and if he had money that was proof enough of respectability. How he came by the cash would never be asked, for it was then an article of the European business community's creed that all Americans were both honest and rich.

And if you're wondering how I came to know all this, let

me say at once that I had picked it up only by word of mouth. I had no idea what a foreign country looked like, and absolutely no personal experience of how foreigners treated Americans. I was making my first ever trip away from my native shores, and I was about to find out a lot of things I didn't know.

2

HOW TO MAKE MONEY IN EUROPE

One May morning shortly after the *Russia* docked I walked into the North- Western Station in Liverpool and took the train for London. The bonds were in a little holdall; I made sure this was the one item of luggage I kept my hands on. Everything going on around me was novel and strange, but like most young people I thought I was the smartest guy around and the rest of the world had better beware.

The train arrived in London in drizzling rain. I took a cab to Langham Place, where I enjoyed a regular English tea. Next night I left Victoria Station for Dover, crossed to Ostend, went through to Brussels and realised a boyhood ambition by visiting the field of Waterloo. When I checked out of the Hotel de Paris in Brussels next day I was stunned at the management's inventiveness in making charges – towels, candles, soap, attendance, paper, envelopes, there seemed no end of them. Fingering my holdall full of stolen bonds, I thought that we all have to make money somehow, even robbing someone else if necessary.

I took the train for Frankfurt, for it was there that I had decided to sell the loot, and I wanted to get it over quickly so I could enjoy myself, look around these famous lands, and relax. Gazing out of the train window, I was shocked – as indeed are most Americans travelling on the Continent – to see women working at dirty jobs. I saw a number of them shovelling coal, handling the shovel like men. I saw women labouring in brickyards too, digging and wheeling clay, and they seemed to be everywhere in the fields doing men's work. I found it all rather repugnant – we would never allow such things to happen back home.

Various strange folk got in and out of the train during the journey, but one old gentleman stayed in my carriage for some time. He started up a conversation about antique collecting, and becoming confidential, produced a box of fine cigars and a bottle of wine.

"What is your vocation in life, sir?" he asked me in perfect English.

"I'm a banker. I'm here to see if there are any prospects of extending my New York business to Europe. And yourself?"

"I'm a plain clothes police officer – actually, chief of the Antwerp secret service."

Well, what do you say to that, I asked myself, tightening my grip on my holdall.

Of course, he thought I was innocent because I was young. He certainly wanted to talk. He told me about the case he was currently on.

"It concerns a rich man named Van Tromp – he's actually a descendant of the famous Dutch Admiral Van Tromp who challenged England's supremacy on the seas during the seventeenth century. Despite the fact he's 70, my Van Tromp met and became infatuated with a German lady named the Countess Elisabeth Winzerode while he was taking the waters at Baden-Baden, which as a well-travelled gentleman you doubtless know is these days the haunt of half the adventurers and adventuresses in Europe searching for a rich victim."

"Of course," I said.

"Did I say infatuated? Is there a stronger word than that? They had only known each other for five days when incredibly he handed over to her half his fortune, and, clearly so that she could get the other half, she agreed to marry him.

"His two daughters tried desperately to prevent the marriage, but they failed. The Countess insisted on honeymooning in Paris, for there, it turned out, she had a former lover, a scoundrel with a criminal record as long as both your arms. Notwithstanding that, the marriage lasted a year, and their first anniversary brought them back to Baden. There Van Tromp thought he'd give his wife a nice surprise by buying her a diamond necklace she coveted. But opening her bedroom door to present it to her he found her in, ahem, how shall I say? a position which could no longer leave him in any doubt about her faithlessness. At which Van Tromp picked up a chair and brought it down on the head of her companion, killing him outright. Then he himself promptly collapsed with a heart attack and died at the foot of the bed. When the will was read he had left everything he possessed to his wife, the Countess Elizabeth."

Hired by the two daughters to investigate the new wife, the detective discovered that this was her third marriage; that her first husband, a Swiss she had married when she was 15, was still alive, and that she was still in touch with him.

"At the moment she is in Cologne," he told me. "I shall leave this train there and find her, and follow her until she meets up with her Swiss husband. The moment I can prove they are married, as they undoubtedly still are, her marriage to Van Tromp can be declared null and void, and so therefore can the will."

As you can imagine, I was fascinated. When the train arrived in Cologne I actually thought for a moment about giving up what I was doing and joining the detective to track down the cunning Countess Elisabeth. Then the absurdity of such an idea struck me, and I shook hands with him and wished him good luck. As I watched him disappearing down the platform I had no idea that one day I was going to meet the Countess Elisabeth Winzerode in most bizarre circumstances. But that is for later. From Cologne to Frankfurt is 140 miles

... it is now five o'clock in the afternoon and we are drawing into the station.

I took a cab to the Hotel Landsberg, and although travel-weary, I went out to see the city sights. That night I couldn't sleep. My mind was buzzing with plans for the days ahead of me.

In London there was an American banking house (it has since gone bankrupt) which was doing big business in issuing letters of credit – or credits, as they were called – without inquiry to anyone applying for them. While I was in London I had called at their office, 449 the Strand, and paying $750 was given a credit for £150, which I took under a false name. I wanted this letter as an introduction to some of the Frankfurt bankers, so as to open the way to negotiate the bonds. The Frankfurt associates of the London firm were Kraut, Launtner and Co., on the Gallogasse. Next morning I went to their offices, produced my letter, was cordially received, and was invited to make my head-quarters in their office during my stay, which for the next day or two I did. But from there I also called on several other bankers, feeling the way, and finally select-ed the firm of Murpurgo and Wiesweiller, widely known and enormously wealthy. When I announced my busi-ness I was invited into a splendid room; the man who rose from a deep leather chair with his hand out-stretched was Herr Murpurgo himself.

"I'm delighted to meet you, Mr. Bidwell," he said. "We rarely have American clients, so it is a special plea-sure. How can we help you?"

"You are most generous," I replied. "I've come to Europe on business because I'm arranging to buy sever-al copper-mines in Austria. If I can close the deal, which I expect to do within the next few days, I shall want to sell a large block of American bonds and use the cash to pay for the mines."

I saw Herr Murpurgo's steely eyes glint. No doubt he thought he could make a good thing out of it.

"Yes, we will buy the bonds as soon as you're ready," he said.

You will recall that as far as the innocent holder of bearer bonds was concerned he was perfectly safe. The downside was that it was still a custom among bankers that whenever bonds were lost by fraud or theft they would send out circulars with the numbers, requesting that anyone offering them should be questioned and held. The upside was that millions of American bonds were being sold freely all over the Continent, and if the seller looked respectable the circulars were unlikely to be checked. But suppose I had misinterpreted the glint in Herr Murpurgo's eyes? I couldn't be too careful, I decided. So after promising to return soon I left his office and went to Wiesbaden, 15 miles away. There I booked into a hotel under another name. My plan was to leave the bonds there, travel into Frankfurt every day, and return to Wiesbaden every evening. Why Wiesbaden? Because at this time it was one of the few places where you could lose your identity, its gambling joints and spa waters had made it, along with Baden-Baden, the Monte Carlo of Germany.

Every day for the next five days I took the train to Frankfurt and back, calling occasionally on Murpurgo and Weissweiller, and spinning them a cock-and-bull tale about the impending purchase of my Austrian copper-mines. On the fourth day I told them the deal was just about certain, so much so that I had ordered the securities I intended to dispose of to be forwarded from London. I gave them a list, and they gave me a memorandum offer for the lot. Next day I handed over the bonds. An unctuous clerk ran his eye over them and then asked me if I would mind waiting.

That wait lasted exactly an hour, a very bad sixty minutes for me. I was convinced they had found out something, that any minute the door would be flung open and in would come the *Polizei*. I need not have worried. All that was happening, it turned out, was that the clerks were simply hurrying around getting the money out of the bank before it closed. When I had been invited to verify all the amounts they had figured up, one of the partners hurried off to the bank and in five minutes he was back with 200,000 gulden. I shook hands warmly with Herr Murpurgo, thanked him for his hospitality and his help, and departed.

I was still nervous. I wanted to put a good distance between me and Frankfurt as fast as I could. I took the train back to Wiesbaden and went straight to the Casino, where I knew they always held a million francs as well as German cash, and where a large sum of money would attract no particular attention. I exchanged my gulden for 350 one-thousand-franc notes, and from there went straight to Rothschild's, where I bought exchange on New York for $80,000. That same night I left for London.

There were no sleeping-cars in Europe in those days, so I sat up in a compartment and really enjoyed the ride, seeing the countryside by moonlight. At midnight we arrived at Calais and took the boat for Dover, followed by the express for London. At Victoria Station I took a cab to Mrs. Green's, where I had breakfast *à l'anglais.*

My stay in London was intended to be brief, but it was lengthened by a little adventure that I got while doing some sight-seeing. On the corner with Bow Street is a famous drinking saloon called the Gaiety, flooded with light inside and out, with more than half a dozen very beautiful barmaids. Barmaids are a great institution in England,they never have more than one man behind a bar, none at all in the railway bars. Every year in London there is a "Beautiful; Barmaid Show" held in some public park; thousands of people flock to see it, and the winners are on to something because they can get big salaries at the better class bar-rooms. Anyway, feeling relaxed after my Continental ordeal, I went into the Gaiety for a drink.

"Hello, sir, my name's Eliza," said my barmaid. "And

what can I get you?"

I asked for a pot of local ale, and at once discovered that my accent held immense interest for Eliza, a real English blue-eyed beauty with ringlets in her hair in the old-fashioned style, and an eye-catching décolletage. The Gaiety wasn't particularly busy that night, so every few minutes she would come over and tell me her life story. She was married but her husband had been caught thieving and was in jail for the rest of his life, "so now I'm neither married nor a widow, which is no state for a woman to be in." She lived close by, in one of those teeming courts that run off from The Strand and when she came off duty at midnight she gratefully accepted my offer to accompany her to her front door. When she kissed me good night her lips lingered just long enough to make me feel that here was a bank at which I was usefully in credit, so I told her that business kept me in London next day, which was far from true, and perhaps we could meet again.

"Oh, Austin, I'd love that," said Eliza. "Tomorrow I'm on early start and I'm free in the evening."

"Then come to dinner!" I said. I hadn't the faintest idea where I might take her, but I arranged to pick her up from the Gaiety. Then she kissed me again, and my credit soared.

Next day I arranged a private room for dinner at a restaurant near the Gaiety, I think it was in a street appropriately called Maiden Lane. When I told the head waiter that I would be bringing a young lady and I hoped it would not inconvenience the establishment if we could be left alone, he replied: "Oh, that's quite in order, sir. As a matter of fact, I can arrange for you to have the room where the Prince of Wales comes regularly to dine with a lady friend. I shall see that after dinner you are left quite alone, and you will find every convenience there."

The Prince of Wales! To be in such exalted company! I gave the man five sovereigns with a careless gesture. I was young, glad to be alive after Frankfurt, and I had other people's money to be liberal with. My merry-eyed Eliza was equally ecstatic when we walked into our very own dining room, all in Regency stripes and dark red velvet.

"The Prince of Wales!" she echoed. "Lord luvus!"

We ate oysters, then game pie, a fine English cheese called Stilton, for which the establishment was apparently renowned, peach melba, and drank lots of champagne which Eliza was soon calling "lubberly bubberly". After the waiter had retired leaving the coffee, she announced, in rather less delicate language than I shall use, that she had noticed my eyes had been riveted on her décolletage "almost since last night when I met you", and she thought the time had come to gratify my curiosity. I felt myself being dragged on to her suddenly revealed bosom and my credit went through the roof. I will leave the rest of that evening to your imagination, but should anyone think I was taking advantage of a poor defenceless girl, let me say that Eliza needed no coaxing, for I really believe she wanted someone to love her for a fleeting hour or so in some place more exotic than a dreary tenement room off the Strand. Indeed, as is so often the case with casual love, we were both using each other, at any rate, I believe I made America as unforgettable for her as she made London unforgettable for me. At four in the morning, back at the front door of her teeming tenement, I gave her my address in New York and urged her to find better work and let me know how she got on. She did find a new job, in an eel-pie shop in Red Lion Square, High Holborn. I saw her again two years later in London, and I am pleased to say she was as generous to me with her favours as she was on that delightful night in our private dining room.

Next day, bug-eyed, I took the train to Liverpool, embarked on the steamer Java, and ten days later we were sailing through the Narrows. All through that voyage I was making up my mind I would go straight. As we went past Staten Island I was preparing a little speech for Irving: "That's it, and no more! I'm turning my back for ever on crime." At the wharf Irving was standing on the edge of the closely packed crowd, watching the steamer with a nervous look on his face. I waved and pointed significantly to my pocket; for answer his faced wreathed in smiles and he cried out, "I'm glad to see you!" I bet you are, I thought.

At the bottom of the gang-plank he came forward, put his arm round my shoulder and said, "Well done! We'll soon have another job for you." I was so stunned that my speech vanished into thin air. Stanley and White were waiting at Taylors Hotel on Montgomery street, a few doors up from the wharf, and they gave me an enthusiastic welcome. I opened my bag and showed them the sixteen bills of exchange for $5,000 each, telling them they would have their cash in ninety minutes. They fingered the bills, passing them to each other, examining them with anxious care, like children. Then I gathered up the paper and went out to a friend of mine, a well-known New Street broker.

"I've just come back from Europe," I said. "Could I ask you to step round the corner with me to the bankers and identify me?"

He was surprised and delighted, sure he would vouch for me. Endorsing the drafts, I told them to make it in five-hundreds; they sent out to the bank for them, and I was soon on my way back to our rendezvous with 160 $500 greenbacks in a roll. My three top cops nearly popped their eyeballs. My share was $10,000, then to show their appreciation they each gave me another $1,000.

In the next few days rumour went round Wall Street that I had just cleared $100,000 in some complex international deal, and a week later people were doffing their hats to me in the street and my waiter at Delmonico's was bowing even lower than was his custom. But money, I was discovering, is a strange thing. Just when you think you've got it, you haven't got it at all.

Let me tell you why. While I was basking in my new-found fame I was also busily paying off my debts. The largest was for $1,300, partly borrowed money and partly a long-standing balance due on a speculation negotiated on my account, and which didn't pan out. Then I indulged pretty freely in some extravagances, like a dozen or so new suits and the like. Two so-called buddies stuck me for a loan; both remain unpaid to this hour, along with 25 years' interest. So within a couple of weeks of my return my $13,000 was down to just about half, and my vision of unbounded wealth was evaporating as fast as my greenbacks. It began to hit me that far from giving up, as I had vowed I would tell Irving I would, I would pretty soon be in need of pulling another job.

As it happened, another job wasn't very far away.

3

A SWINDLER AT THE BAR

By the time he was 40, Edwin James Q.C. had pushed his way from the bottom of the legal profession to the topmost height of the English Bar, and was already singled out to become the next Attorney-General. Only one step remained to place him where his ultimate destiny seemed to lie – the seat of the Lord Chancellor.

But you won't find Edwin James anywhere in English history books.

For at about the same time – the year is 1865 – dark whispers were circulating through the London clubs that despite the fact that his income was nearer twenty thousand pounds a year than ten, James was heavily in debt. The reason was twofold. First, as was generally known, he was keeping two houses, one which his beautiful wife presided over, and the other where his equally beautiful mistress reigned. And second, he was losing large sums at his club at baccarat and loo.

Among James' clients was a fast young aristocratic buck, heir to an historic name and a great estate. Like James himself, this client was also heavily in debt, but was successfully bridging the gap between his income and expenditure by raising loans from moneylenders. These sharks were only too eager to lend the young blood money on what are known in English law as post-obits, which then carried the trifling interest of about 100 per cent a year. A post-obit is a form of note or due bill given by the heir of an estate, which matures the moment the drawer of the document enters into that estate. That is to say, the son discounts his father's death to provide fuel to feed his flame.

It occurred to Edwin James that his young client was issuing so many post-obits that by the time he came into his fortune he would never know within a good many thousands how much he had borrowed in his reckless youth, or even the number of post-obits he had given. This idea came to him because as the young rake's lawyer, he took charge of all his affairs, even acting as intermediary between his client and the usurers, collecting cash from them and passing it on to his client. So James did something that no future Lord Chancellor could possibly afford to do – he made out two post-obits each of £5,000 on his client's behalf, forged his client's signature, and pocketed the cash himself to pay his own debts.

But the parasitic Edwin James reckoned without his host, who was made of keener stuff than many imagined. To the ultimate surprise of all who knew him, the young prodigal kept his books arrow-straight, and knew to a single guinea how much and to whom he was owing. When his father died the various post-obits were put in front of him, and he instantly declared that the two signed by Edwin James were forgeries. The crime was laid at the QC's door without difficulty. While the gossip spread through the clubrooms and to the newspapers (where the story was published under the thinly disguised alias of "a distinguished member of the Bar,") the new lord, as he had now become, announced that he would not prosecute if the criminal left England; that is to say, if James failed to exile himself he would be arrested and arraigned at the Old Bailey.

James of course fled. New York was then as good a place as any for a fugitive from justice, and having arrived there he struck up a rapid acquaintance with Richard O'Gorman, a prominent New York lawyer, and applied through him for admission to the city's Bar. The story of the English lawyer's crime had preceded him to

New York, so that there was some bitter opposition to his application, until it was known that the much-revered O'Gorman was his champion. Then many began to feel that after all the poor fellow should perhaps be given another chance. The rest were won over, a decision they would one day regret, when O'Gorman brought all his splendid eloquence into play to support James' candidature at a meeting of the New York Bar Association.

James was duly elected, but he failed lamentably in his efforts to secure an American practice. The best he could do was get himself a back room in a building on Broadway, facing the City Hall, with a sign on the door which said "Edwin James, Counselor-at-Law and Register in Bankruptcy." In the grey light of day the effects of O'Gorman's eloquence had faded away; James' professional associates looked upon him with suspicion, and there was a general impression among them that his criminal activities might not be wholly behind him. For all that, he managed to endear himself to the press and the general public. He appeared as an unpaid defence counsel in two or three murder cases and his powerful speeches to the courts attracted considerable notice in the papers.

His professional colleagues had got it right though. The Englishman had continued his extravagant ways and within a year of his arrival in New York he was desperate for cash to meet his creditors, to such an extent that he was having to leave his house before daybreak and return to it only at night. This was just at the time when I returned from Europe on the mission for my three top cops.

"We will soon have another job for you!" Jimmy Irving had said. And a week or two later: "I'd like you to meet Edwin James, Austin. He's a good friend of mine and he'd like to do some business with you."

I knew as soon as I heard the "business" briefly explained, that I would need some help, so I decided to enlist a friend of long standing, George Macdonnell, who was always plain "Mac" to me. Mac was an intellectual genius. He spoke several languages fluently, no problem was too big for him, and he had that sense of wonder about all things on earth that made his sparkling conversation and his shrewd observations a delight to listen to. I honestly believe that he could have been destined for fame at whatever he chose to do; as it was, he was destined only for infamy, as will be revealed. The day after I was introduced to Edwin James I went to his office by appointment, and Mac came with me.

Another man, introduced to us as Louis Brea, was already waiting there. James was sitting behind his large polished desk, riffling through a bundle of papers. As soon as we were comfortable he began to outline the deal.

Louis Brea, it seemed, had married the second daughter of a wealthy but not over-respectable New York family named Farrell. The family's lawyer was Edwin James, who had drawn the will of the mother, a dreadful, hot-tempered woman who would use her fists or any other weapon to achieve her ends. Her husband, the father of Brea's wife, and creator of the Farrell fortune, was dead, so the vast family property in securities, stocks and land was vested absolutely in the irascible mother.

James pulled a paper from the heap on his desk and tapped it with his forefinger.

"This is the will," he said. "You will notice that in it Mrs. Farrell has left her second daughter, Mrs. Brea, the sum of just one dollar; in other words, she has discarded her. This is entirely in keeping with her character, and she is not likely to change her mind."

To correct this obviously unfair state of affairs, unfair, that is, to Brea, as he saw it, Brea and James had between them drafted another will, in which Mrs. Brea was down for legacies amounting to $750,000. The plan was that as soon as Mrs. Farrell went to meet her maker

James would produce the second will and destroy the genuine one.

"Mrs. Farrell is very old and very frail," James told us, passing over the second will for our inspection. "When she dies we are prepared to pay you $100,000 out of the proceeds so long as this second will is not disputed, which is very unlikely. For this consideration, I shall require $5,000 in cash from you within the next fourteen days."

In a nutshell, James was skint. He had to have five grand to pay his creditors, and the way he thought he might get it without any trouble to himself was to cut us in on his crooked deal with Louis Brea.

Well, I liked it, and so did Mac. "It'll be like buying ourselves a pension," Mac said as we talked it over afterwards in a Broadway coffee shop. It didn't take us long to work out how to get the cash James needed. We set to and hired an empty office downtown under a false company name, then we took on a simple, unsuspicious fellow as porter and messenger. I ferreted around getting the low-down on companies banking with the mighty firm of Jay Cooke and Co., corner of Wall and Nassau Streets. When I had sufficient information Mac, whose talents included wonderful artistic skills (particularly useful in copying cheques and signatures) got to work with pens and inks.

Four days after we'd moved into our office our messenger walked into Jay Cooke's with a cheque for $20,000 purporting to be signed by another firm who banked with them. Along with the cheque went a letter bearing a signature well known to the cashier, asking him to pay the cheque to bearer. Five minutes later we sent a message to Edwin James telling him to meet us at Delmonico's, corner of Broadway and Chambers Street. We got to the restaurant first, he came in shortly afterwards. After we shook hands I produced a roll of ten five-hundreds, fresh out of Jay Cooke's. James positively beamed. He didn't know about the other fifteen grand, of course, which, after a few deductions, was for our expenses and our pains. I paid off our messenger with a small gift, and slipped $2,000 to Jimmy Irving for the contact.

"We ought to be able to make the rest of the cash last until Mrs. Farrell pops and we collect the $100,000," Mac said. But it didn't work out like that. Winter passed and the hot New York summer was already half-way through. Far from popping, the old termagant whose heirs we now were seemed to renew her youth, and threatened to outlive us all.

During this time I had taken on my brother George as a partner in my routine financial business. Now George was a thinking fellow, and when he heard our story of the will he shook his head censoriously.

"That's a scoundrelly business, robbing the heirs of an estate," he said. "And look at what Brea and James are getting out of it, compared to yourselves."

Mac and I looked at each other, each aware of what the other was thinking: George was right, we weren't doing as well out of it as we should.

"I suggest you chuck out James and Brea," George went on. "But first, you can make use of them both like this." He drew up a chair and swiftly outlined the plot.

George's idea required the co-operation of Jimmy Irving and his police force, which was no problem, since Irving would be cut in for 25 per cent. It also required the use of James' office, for a cash considera-tion to him. It meant, however, that the lawyer would not be able to escape questioning and a considerable degree of suspicion, to the point that it would put an end to any lingering remnants of character he had on hand or in stock. That, as it turned out, didn't much matter, because in the years that had passed James had grown tired of America. When we told him about George's plan he almost at once said he would vamoose to Paris with his share of the plunder.

With the details all worked out, we were set to go. We

had audaciously decided that lightning would strike once more in the same place – that is, Jay Cooke were to be the victims again. So for starters we sent Louis Brea to the firm's Philadelphia headquarters, where by a mixture of bravado and finesse, he procured from no less a person than Jay Cooke himself an introduction to the manager of the New York branch.

Meanwhile, I had discovered details of a Newark manufacturer named Newman who had recently gone bust. On the morning after his triumphant return from Philadelphia, Brea presented himself at James' office, it being arranged that James should be out, telling the clerk that his name was Newman, that he had lately failed in business, and wanted Mr. James to act for him in the bankruptcy court.

"Sir," said the clerk. "I'm sure Mr. James would be happy to meet you. If you come back at midday, you will find him in."

At 12 James came, and the clerk introduced Brea as Newman. James made a point of keeping the clerk conveniently near him, so that he could hear the ensuing conversation. Brea, as Newman, then told James he had spent in his business $240,000 belonging to his wife and mother, and that in rescheduling his assets he proposed to use enough to make those amounts good, and that he would conceal the fact from his creditors. He was determined to invest the amount in bonds, so ran his story, and was going to deposit the money in the bank that afternoon. At this point he produced his letter of introduction from Jay Cooke.

All this was, of course, a charade played out for the eye and ear of the clerk, who might later be called as a witness of his employer's good faith.

Still in the presence of the clerk, Brea-Newman said to James: "I propose to pay you a retaining fee of $250. I wonder if I might ask you to introduce me to your bank, as I shall want a small credit handy."

James stroked his chin thoughtfully. "That will be difficult," he said. "My bank is in Jersey City."

James and Brea both knew that the clerk's brother was paying teller at the New York branch of the Chemical Bank. Just as they expected, up piped the clerk: "Let me introduce Mr. Newman to the Chemical Bank."

"Excellent idea," responded James. And off went Brea-Newman with the clerk, returning in ten minutes with a cheque-book in his pocket and $5,000 to his credit at the bank.

The same afternoon Brea-Newman presented his letter of introduction at Jay Cooke's and told an entirely different story to the manager there.

"An uncle has died and left me his very considerable fortune," he said. "I'm realising on my real estate and buying bonds as fast as the money comes in. Eventually I want to put a million dollars into railway bonds. At the moment I have $240,000 on hand, which I want to invest in government bonds."

The manager was of course only too delighted to help. Brea looked good, was sartorially splendid, and talked in a refined New England way. But at this stage Brea wanted only to make an impression. He would be back, he said, leaving the manager in no doubt that here was good business indeed.

In the next three or four days Brea paid several visits to the Chemical Bank, getting small cheques certified for $500 and $1,000, until his account was drawn down to $1,000. Then he saw the manager again and told him he would take his $240,000 in seven-thirties, bearer bonds, and he'd call next day and pay for them. Would they give him a pro-forma bill for them? They would be only too delighted.

When the eventful day came James sent his clerk on an errand to the Admiralty Court to get him out of the way. At 10 a.m. Brea sent a messenger with a note to the bankers, asking them to send the bonds to Edwin James' office, and he would pay for them on delivery. He was sorry he couldn't come himself, he was in consultation with the executors of his late uncle's estate.

Brea then signed two cheques. The first was for $240,000, the full value of the bonds. He put this one in his pocket. It was drawn on the Chemical Bank and was similar to cheques always given between bankers on bond transactions. The second cheque, also drawn on the Chemical Bank, was for $240. The funds in Brea's account existed to meet this amount, of course. Brea put this cheque in his hatband.

When the bank messenger arrived with the bonds, Brea-Newman was going to say: "I've got the cheque for them here. We'll take the bonds to the Chemical Bank and get them to certify my cheque." At the bank he would take out both cheques, letting the messenger get a glimpse of the large one only. He would pass the small one in through the window asking for it to be certified. When that was done and the cheque returned, Brea would surreptitiously change it and hand the messenger the big one. We would then have the bonds, and the bank would have a dud cheque.

It sounded infallible, and it would have been but for one thing. To explain, I have to go back to the night before.

We had met in James' office to polish the final details, and satisfied that everyone knew their parts, we adjourned to the uptown Delmonico's for dinner. It so happened that at the next table was Detective George Elder, of the New York Police. This Elder was a bright fellow with his own ring, his own bank account, diamond pin and rig for the road. I knew him vaguely, but none of the others did. I had my back to him, and didn't even know he was there until much later. Unfortunately, our table finished eating and left before his, and to pile on the misfortune Brea left some papers on the table, among them the pro-forma bill for the bonds given him by the bankers. Perhaps for security reasons, he had already torn off the heading bearing the name of the firm and the purchaser and destroyed it.

Elder picked it up, and thinking vaguely that there must be a plot somewhere, decided to make inquiries of the hundred or more bankers and brokers in Wall Street. He did this without informing his immediate superior, which was also unfortunate for us, because his immediate superior was Jimmy Irving, who, seeing his percentage in jeopardy, would have quietly crushed him. The trouble with the New York Police Department was that the whole force was split into cliques, each one jealous of all the others, each with its own patch, and each strictly protecting its own territory.

Elder, the fragment of pro-forma bill in his hand, started his inquiries at 9.30 a.m. He had been at it for just over an hour when he walked into Jay Cooke's offices, just as the messenger was leaving for James' office with the bonds. Fifteen more minutes and we'd have made it, but it wasn't to be. Elder produced the pro-forma bill and waved it in front of the manager.

"Have you seen this before?" he asked.

"Yes. It's one of ours."

"Do you know the man you gave it to? Are you sure it's all right?"

"It's quite in order, officer. It belongs to Mr. Newman, who was introduced to us by the president of our firm in Philadelphia. But I must say it's strange that the bill should have been torn like this."

"You know what I think, sir? I think there's a fraud intended here."

The manager's jaw dropped. If there was a fraud, he didn't need that kind of publicity. Turning to the messenger, who was almost at the door with our bonds, he said: "You wait here with the police officer. I'll go round and talk to Mr. Newman."

When the manager arrived at James' office Brea was there anxiously awaiting the messenger's arrival, his two cheques at the ready. Mac, George and I were in another room, listening behind the closed door. As soon as he saw the manager, James knew the game was up, for any suspicion as to good faith was fatal to our success. The manager strode in, shook "Mr. Newman's" hand, told him the bonds would arrive soon, and added: "I suppose you don't mind paying cash for them?"

Brea, his heart suddenly sinking like a pit lift, replied coolly: "Certainly. I'll go to my bank with you now if you like. They'll certify my cheque for the amount and give you the cash. Or perhaps you'd like to leave it until the messenger comes with the bonds."

This offer seemed totally to disarm the manager, who must have thought that Detective Elder had got it hopelessly wrong.

"All right," he said. "I'll send the messenger to your bank with you." He went to the door, turned and added: "Draw the cash from your bank, Mr. Newman, and pay the messenger in notes when he gives you the bonds."

As the door closed behind him Mac, George and I came out from our separate office and agreed with Brea and James that we'd blown it, and the only thing left to do now was to try to shield James. For the time being Brea would have to lie low. He left the office hurriedly, first instructing the clerk to tell the messenger when he came that he had gone for the money, and would call for the bonds. When the messenger arrived, accompanied by Detective Elder, there was of course, no Brea, so the bonds were taken back again.

That afternoon James called at the bankers, where he was well known.

"Have you seen Mr. Newman?" he asked the manager. "He's arranged to meet me here."

"He certainly isn't here, sir," replied the manager. Then, as James expected, he added: "I wonder if you'd care to come into my office and have a word with me, Mr. James."

In the inner sanctum the manager asked: "I have to confess we are rather mystified by Mr. Newman. Do you have any personal knowledge of him?"

"I'm simply his legal adviser, that's all," James said. "He called on me a while ago, paid me a small retaining fee, and we haven't progressed much from there. I'm afraid I can't vouch for him at all."

The manager produced a telegram. "I've had this from our head office in Philadelphia. It's in reply to one I sent them, asking if his letter of introduction was genuine or not. As you can see, they say the introduction is genuine, but they know absolutely nothing about the man and they suggest I should proceed with care in his affairs."

"Good gracious!" gasped James. "This may be serious. If he doesn't arrive soon for his appointment with me I shall begin to suspect him too."

Mr. Newman did not, of course, turn up, leaving James and the bank manager congratulating each other on probably having escaped from a fraudster.

"I shall give this story to the press," declared the manager, adding: "I will of course, ensure that your name is not mentioned."

The irony of that was that had we successfully stung the bank, they would have moved heaven and earth to ensure the story never leaked out. But now the case was different. All the morning papers had long and absurdly inaccurate accounts of the transaction, in which the manager was portrayed as a commercial genius, and the unfortunate Elder – who both expected and deserved all the glory – wasn't even mentioned.

James cleared his debts with the $5,000 we gave him, but he never did get to Paris. He managed to hold on somehow, hoping to realise on Mrs. Farrell's will. By the time she had a fatal heart attack after a particularly vicious outbreak of temper four years later, the Englishman was hopelessly in debt. Eagerly James now donned his mantle of family lawyer and produced and read Mrs. Farrell's last will and testament. Brea's wife Sarah was stunned when she heard she was chief heir to the estate. The rest of the family sat gaping at each other in shocked disbelief.

It never occurred to the other three sisters to contest the will, but it did occur to a nephew, a poor relation named Eagan, who received a legacy of $500, an amount he regarded as being so derisory that he loudly declared that he wouldn't put up with it. Off he went and hired a briefless lawyer named Abraham Ezra, who was determined to make his way in the world, and told him he wanted to contest the will.

Louis Brea meantime couldn't wait for probate to be completed before maximising his wife's great fortune, and moved at once into his dead mother-in-law's mansion. No sooner was his last stick of furniture in place than the executors of the will – they were two simple shopkeepers, the same in the forged will as in the genuine one – were told by the lawyer Ezra of his client's intentions, and warned to dispossess Brea of the house until the law decreed it to be his wife's property. Knowing James by reputation, Ezra then decided on a hunch to stick his neck out a long way, declaring: "I strongly believe the will is a forgery."

At this point while the three sisters were still not hostile to him, Brea should have struck a deal with Ezra. Instead he unwisely called the lawyer a shyster and a blackmailer.

Ezra didn't like being called those sort of names, and his blood was up. He frightened the three sisters into supporting him in disputing the will, and insisted they return to live in the mansion. Too late Brea now tried to negotiate. Ezra almost certainly could have been bought off, had he not started paying court to the youngest of the sisters, Jane. Past 30 and without any accomplishments, she had never been wooed before, and quickly made Ezra her hero, investing the thin-shanked, narrow-chested, waspish attorney with a thousand tender attributes. A month later his offer of marriage had her declaring she was the most favoured woman in the world, and in the middle of their happy lovers' talk in the old library she ran to a shelf, took down a book, opened it, and revealed a soiled sheet of paper.

"I found this in a book the other day," said simple Jane. "It's in mother's writing. What does it mean?"

It was the draft of a new will, in Mrs. Farrell's own handwriting, boldly signed and dated the night of her death. Ezra knew that even without witnesses it would stand up in court. When he kissed his love a tender good night and went home, he hardly felt the paving stones under his feet, for tucked away in the pocket of his waistcoat, just over his heart, was the little soiled piece of paper which told him in unmistakable terms that his fortune was made. For the will reiterated the legacy of just one dollar to Sarah, Brea's wife, and split the rest of the fortune between Jane and her other two sisters.

Unfortunately for Brea, before the discovery of the new will, he and Sarah had borrowed in a big way from the banks, getting plenty of credit because she was an heiress. As soon as the truth was out the creditors became clamorous. Unable to pay, Brea was arrested on civil suits, and languished in jail for six months until, on Ezra's advice the three sisters said they would meet all his debts and give him and his wife $1,000 each, provided they agreed to live west of Chicago.

Louis and Sarah Brea went to Montana. They opened a saloon in Butte City, but Brea never recovered his spirits again. What destroyed him was not so much the fact that he became his own saloon's best customer but that he had been in full possession of the mansion for three weeks and had spent hours alone in the old library, and yet hadn't discovered and destroyed the new will lying there.

The saloon failed, and ruined in pocket, health and character, he was left bare to every storm that blew. One fine morning as the sun was rising over the town half a dozen all-night gamblers in a neighbouring saloon got up to leave, and as they passed through the doorway they almost fell over the body of a man, ragged, emaciated, forlorn. It was Louis Brea.

As for Edwin James, as soon as he'd read the forged will to the family he had characteristically cajoled $5,000 out of Brea "on account". When the thunderbolt of the new will fell, sadly recognising that he would shake hands with fortune no longer, he fled to London, where a few years later he died in extreme poverty. Thus the man who was tipped to join the illustrious line of Lord Chancellors which included Thomas 'a Becket and Cardinal Wolsey, and who might have been buried in Westminster Abbey, was instead laid to rest in a pauper's grave.

Now, however, I must return you to what appeared to be the ruin of our lives, staring at us after our plot was discovered and Brea could no longer collect the bonds on which our hopes of fortune lay. This was my second successive failure; I could not afford another. If I was to become as rich as I intended, I had to make crime pay. As Louis Brea was vanishing into the streets of New York I sat down with Mac and George, drew pen and paper towards me, and drew up a plan.

"This scheme is absolutely time-critical," I said. "And it will require that all three of us travel to Europe."

4

CASH COUPS IN FRANCE AND GERMANY

We landed in Liverpool in the highest spirits and took the train for London, enjoying the novelty of everything.

I suppose we felt carefree and cavalier because the moments of high tension were yet to come, but we had two good reasons to feel pleased with ourselves. First was the bundle of forged letters of credit we were carrying, all drawn on the Union Bank of London. Mac, our master forger, had worked for a month producing them in New York. George and I had studied them critically in artificial light and in daylight, and we both agreed that so long as they weren't checked with the Union Bank before we had drawn cash on them, any European banker was bound to accept they were genuine.

Our second reason for feeling good was that before we left New York we had done a deal with Police Captain Jimmy Irving. If any of us were arrested in Europe the first people the police would check us out with would be the New York police. Irving and his acolytes would then solemnly declare that we were men of the highest standing on Wall Street, without a stain on our characters, that a terrible mistake must have been made and that we should be released before a major international incident arose out of it. For this guaranteed protection we would pay Irving 10 per cent of our gross profits.

We had already decided that George would go to

France, to Bordeaux, Marseilles and Lyons; and Mac and I would go to Germany, to Berlin, Munich, Leipzig and Frankfurt. We crossed the Channel together on a Saturday boat, and at Calais George said goodbye and started south for Bordeaux, while we took the train eastwards for Berlin.

Five days later we were back in London, each with our stories to tell. This, in George's own words, is what happened to him.

"After leaving you in Calais I arrived in Bordeaux via Paris, booked in to the Hotel d'Orient, and, after a bath and breakfast went to the bankers. As soon as they saw my letters of introduction I was received with beaming smiles. They invited me to dinner, wanted to drive me through their city, all of which I said I had to decline as my agent was waiting for me at Bayonne, where I'd bought some land and property. But, I added, I would be happy if they would cash my draft for £2,000 and endorse it on my letter of credit.

"This seemed to nonplus the manager. It was the custom of French bankers, he said, to require twenty-four hours before drawing a cheque – would the next day do?

"'We shall be happy to assist you,' he said, 'in passing the time pleasantly.'

"This was something I hadn't bargained for. I declined, saying I really had to get to Bayonne on business that night.

"'I suppose,' I said, 'your people won't mind your checking out a small sum without the usual notice. But if it's embarrassing for you I can easily go elsewhere.'

"The manager didn't want that to happen. 'I'll see what I can do,' he said, and went off, leaving me with a couple of his staff. I knew that the least show of haste or anxiety would betray me, but I have to confess I was mighty worried that they might have sent a despatch to London and were delaying me while they waited for a reply. Then – relief! Here was the manager come back with the full sum in French banknotes. I slowly counted out the 50,000 francs, and took my leave.

"As we had agreed, I sent all the money by post to the Queen's Hotel, London, so that it would be safe if anything happened to me. I wrote on the envelope *"Echantillons de papier"* (paper samples).

"The train for Marseilles didn't leave for another three hours, so in order to reduce the risk I hired a cab and told the driver to take me towards the next station on the way to Marseilles. There I got on the train, and arrived early next morning. I had breakfast at the Hotel d'Europe and looked over the papers to see if the Bordeaux fraud had been discovered. There were no reports about it, so I took a carriage and went to call on Messrs Brune and Co.

"I was again received with great courtesy, and Mr. Brune himself rode with me in the carriage to his bank to effect the sale of my draft on London for £2,500. At the bank he went into the manager's room to introduce the transaction, so I sat on a seat in the front office. The clerks seemed to be eyeing me suspiciously, but I told myself not to worry, they were probably only curious because they could see I was a foreigner. But after Mr. Brune had been gone for a few minutes, the bank porter suddenly stepped to the outer door, closed it and locked it. It was only midday, so I thought, they've found me out, the Bordeaux swindle has been telegraphed all over France. It was only when most of the bank staff left that I realised they were all going off to what seemed to me to be a very early lunch.

"A quarter of a hour later back came Mr. Brune with his hands full of banknotes, putting an end to the hurricane raging inside me.

"'Here you are, Mr. Bidwell,' he said. 'You had better count this lot before you leave the bank's premises. You should find 62,000 francs here.'

"I did, and we drove to my hotel, where we shook hands and parted. I posted the money, *echantillons de papier* again, and again because there was a long wait for the train to Lyons I got a cabbie to drive me to the next station up the line. Even there I still had a long wait, so I drove to a hotel on the seashore and had dinner in a restaurant overlooking the bay.

"Back at the station I bought a ticket for Lyons, but stopped off at Arles, which is a town I always wanted to see. At midnight I took another train from there, and got to Lyons at nine the next morning. I had breakfast at the Hotel de Lyons, checked out the newspapers again and then set about my third and final mission, at the Lyons offices of Messrs. Coudert and Co.

"As soon as I introduced myself Mr. Coudert said, 'Mr. Bidwell, a telegram arrived here for you this morning.' I opened the telegram nonchalantly, well aware of its contents, because I had sent it from Arles the previous evening, addressed to myself at Coudert's to await collection.

"'Ah,' I said, making a show of reading the telegram and then handing it to him. 'You will see that the property transaction I have been arranging in Marseilles is now ready for completion. I shall need 60,000 francs, and I would appreciate it if you could cash a draft on my letter of credit for that amount.'

"This was no problem for the nice Mr. Coudert. He went at once to the safe, took out a bundle of 1,000-franc notes, and counting out sixty, gave them to me.

"I felt certain that by now the Bordeaux fraud must have been discovered, so I reckoned it was time to get out fast, via Paris and Calais. But it occurred to me that the direct Lyons-Paris train might be risky. So I took a carriage back to a junction towards Marseilles, and from there took a train which intersects farther to the north with another line leading through Lyons to Paris. This roundabout route brought me back to Lyons on a night train heading for Paris, where I arrived next day, which was Sunday. I checked in at a small hotel, and shaved off my beard, leaving by the back way. Even so, I decided I would be putting my neck on the block if I took the express to Calais, or even if I bought a ticket direct to Calais or London. I took instead the midday stopping train to Arras, intending to get the Calais train from there.

"There was another long wait at Arras, so I went to a hotel for lunch. Strolling through the little town afterwards, I spoke to some children, who were so delightful that I bought them some sweets. A crowd of them gathered around me, and I realised I might be attracting too much attention. If a local gendarme were to get suspicious, ask questions, take me in .... I had to get rid of my Pied Piper following quickly. Fortunately as I walked along the road, followed by my youthful entourage, I came to the gates of the town cemetery. With a *'Restez ici, mes enfants,'* I went inside. At the back of the cemetery I clambered over a stone wall, slipped, and landed in the middle of a peasant's cabbage patch. The surprised fellow let forth a torrent of abuse which I halted in mid-stream by holding up a five-franc piece. From being my enemy he now became my best friend, and led me down a narrow *ruelle* to the station. I bought a ticket for Calais, crossed the Channel with no mishaps, and here I am."

In his three days in France George had made £7,000, good business by any standards. It was for Mac and I to do at least as well.

They say that the test of a good friend is whether you'd like to travel with them. I had never travelled alone with Mac before, and I soon discovered that I would not have found a more agreeable companion anywhere in the world. With his brilliant scholarship, elegant speech, logical force and fiery enthusiasm he was spellbinding to listen to. With Mac nothing was too big, nothing too little. To him, a thought grasped by the mind of an infant was as wonderful and as much a revelation of God's power as the arch of stars in the Milky Way. While we sped through Belgium and on to the Rhine he was enduringly fascinating until the sun broke the horizon. To hear him tell of the dignity and grace of every human soul and his sure faith that all would be garnered in the mighty plains of heaven, while our baggage was stuffed with forged documents with which we planned to plunder the German banks, was an experience I will never forget.

His oration was finally halted by our arrival in Berlin soon after dark. Mac went to the Hotel Lion de Paris and registered, while I waited across the street in the shadow of the Empress Palace. When he came out we went to have dinner in a large cafe, marvelling at the intensely militaristic scene all around us; I have never seen so many soldiers in a city.* At midnight we parted, I to an obscure hotel, he to the Lion de Paris, arranging our breakfast meeting for eight o'clock in the morning.

When an honest man makes a mistake he can usually pick himself up again. With a villain a mistake can be made easily enough, and it's almost always fatal. We feared the unseen and the unexpected, and planned meticulously to eliminate them. During breakfast Mac went carefully through his pockets, taking out every scrap of paper and turning everything over to me, except of course the documents he needed in the bank. We decided not to fix the amount he should ask for, but agreed that it should not be less than 25,000 gulden, which was $10,000. If everything seemed favourable he was to use his own judgement and go for any sum under 100,000 gulden. His letter of credit was for £10,000, and we didn't want to leave it behind. If we drew any smaller sum than £10,000 the sum would be endorsed on the letter, and it would be returned to Mac.

In Germany the banks open at 9 o'clock, and we knew that soon after 8 a.m. they would receive the letter we had posted from London. We all decided it would be

---

* This was 1872, and Berlin was the capital of Prussia, largest state in the German Empire. By defeating France in a few months in the Franco-Prussian War of 1870-71, the German Empire, created by Bismarck in January 1871, had emerged as the Continent's most powerful military nation.

best for Mac to enter the bankers at about five past nine. So at about 8.45 he got up from the table and I followed, keeping him in sight at a distance of about 100 yards. We went down Unter den Linden, walked across a square and then another couple of blocks, which took Mac to the steps of the bank. I watched him saunter up them and disappear from view.

In Europe money transactions are, for an American, carried out with exasperating slowness, so I settled down grimly to a long wait. In order to reduce my anxiety by even half a minute we had arranged that when he came out if he had the money he was to signal success by stroking his beard. If it was all right, but delayed, he was to put a handkerchief to his face, but if everything went wrong he was to clasp his hands across his chest for a moment.

If that happened I was to keep a lookout to see if he was followed. If he was, I was to give him a signal, at which he would go straight to his hotel, change his clothes, then go out the back way to a shop where I would be waiting. Then we would take a cab to Jüterbog, six miles away, where all trains stopped, and make a fast getaway.

I stationed myself in a little shop across the street, opposite the bank, and settled down for what I guessed would be a weary, anxious watch. The traffic rattled past in both directions and the street thronged with pedestrians, every other one of whom was a soldier, and all of them seemingly arrogant and cocksure, no doubt over their recent conquest of France. I wished I could share their happiness with life right then, for my heart was beating faster by the minute. Suddenly Mac emerged from the bank, smiling and stroking his beard. I followed him, and catching him four or five hundred yards from the bank he simply said "£2,600", and thrust a big packet of gulden notes into my hand.

We separated at once. I went to a number of brokers' offices in the vicinity, buying French francs and gold for nearly the full amount. When we met up again we went to a hatter's and bought Mac one of those broad-brimmed German student hats, which with a pair of spectacles and his beard newly parted in the middle made such a difference that I hardly recognised him.

I found a cabbie and hired him *"zu fahren mich und meinen Freund nach Jüterbog."* Our next objective was Munich, and as the train didn't leave until 12.30 p.m. we had a pleasant drive ahead of us. The cabbie kept us highly amused. From time to time he would take out a loaf of black bread and cut off two slices, one for himself and one for his horse. Seeing we were in no hurry, he would get down and walk beside the horse, feeding himself and the animal at the same time. He was a stupid-looking, crabbed old fellow, but he sure did love that horse.

At Jüterbog we had an hour to spare, so we drove to an inn, ordered a bottle of Hochheimer for ourselves and beer and pretzels for our driver. While no one was looking we put a lighted match to Mac's letter of credit, then each of us went by separate ways to the station booking office, and at 12.30 we boarded the train for Munich.

It was quite late at night when we arrived. Even so, there was time to take in a variety show, which was very Bavarian, with lots of lederhosen, swilling beer and shouting. After the show we separated for the night, each going to a different hotel. The plan was to finish with Munich by 10 a.m. next day, Tuesday, and then make for Leipzig, arriving the same day, then leaving the city that night so that we would be in Frankfurt the following day, Wednesday. As soon as we had done Frankfurt we would make for the safety of London as fast as possible.

Tuesday. At 7 a.m. we breakfasted in a restaurant. Three hours later we had exactly duplicated our Berlin experience. Mac had asked for, and been given, only 12,000 gulden (£1,000), for we had reckoned that to ask for more in this comparatively uncommercial city might have caused difficulties. Although the amount was in gulden, the bank had unfortunately paid him in New Saxon thalers, the thaler being about 70 U. S. cents. We didn't like these thaler notes, but there was no time to change them. Mac put on his specs and his student hat, and parted his beard in the middle again, and just in time we caught the Leipzig train. We sat apart in the same compartment and arrived just after lunch.

At Leipzig the famous trade fair was in full blast. The city overflowed with the fair, a feature of its history for four centuries. There were buyers and sellers from all over the world, even from Russia, and the banks were paying out and receiving money in thousands. What a missed chance! We ought to have had three or four letters to as many banks. Mac sauntered away from the station up a street through the milling crowd to a wine bar, where I joined him. He scrutinised his forged letters carefully, put them in his pocket and went across the road to the bank. From outside I could see the place was full of customers, so I went in too, and stood with the crowd, anxiety seeping through me again.

Mac could have done his business with the first employee who approached him, but that wasn't his way. Instead he asked to see the head of the firm and was shown in with a royal flourish. Producing his letters he asked for 50,000 gulden and probably because at that season in Leipzig that wasn't a large sum, he got it at once. As soon as he came back to the wine bar I went off and changed my New Saxon thalers for French francs and gold. By the time I got back Mac was transformed into a German student again. We were back at the station at 5 p.m., but we had a tedious journey through the night, and didn't arrive in Frankfurt until 10 o'clock next morning.

In Frankfurt 10 a.m. is the time the Bourse opens, and it closes at 2 p.m. For those four hours you won't find any banker in his office, they're all out there on the

Exchange. If we were to do business with the firm to which our letters were addressed, we had perforce to wait until after their late lunch, which began at 2 p.m. That meant possibly 3 or 4 in the afternoon.

This was a situation which was as critical as it was unforeseen. Today was Wednesday, and the third day since our fraud in Berlin. The first draft drawn on London, if promptly posted, might have been delivered at the Union Bank in London this morning. It needed only the manager of the foreign department there to find a draft for a large sum drawn by a stranger and made payable to their correspondent in Berlin for the balloon to go up. He would suspect fraud and would cable Berlin. From there it would probably fly with a thousand exaggerations to every Bourse in Europe.

Dare we then risk waiting until mid-afternoon?

So far we had picked up $43,000 in two days. This money, in notes and gold, was safely in my care, there was no need to post the cash on to London because Mac had done all the "front" work; no one had seen me in any bank, so I could carry the cash on me. But Frankfurt was our big fish. Because it was the money centre of the Continent, its bankers were used to handling large sums, we could within reason have got anything we asked for. Too late again, we realised we ought to have taken Frankfurt first, and left the town with $50,000.

"I think we shouldn't take the risk," I said to Mac, while we sipped our black coffees.

"I don't mind the risk," he replied. "I'm happy to wait until four o'clock and make a dash for Cologne as soon as we've got the cash. The Germans are very thorough, but they're also very slow, and they might not have thought of using the telegraph."

Then, seeing me continuing to weigh the odds, he added: "You're the manager. You make the decision."

"So be it," I said. "We're through. We quit now, have lunch, and head for London."

We took out all our letters, and every scrap of paper relating to them, and went into the men's room. Five minutes later they were all in shreds and flushed down the toilet. In view of the fact that we had far from exhausted our letters of credit, this may seem a strange thing to have done. But let me explain. The amount of cash we drew from each bank was of course endorsed on our letters of credit. If we had been arrested in Europe, under the laws of most European countries they could have convicted us on the verbal statement of the banker, but in America to convict one of forgery the document itself must be produced in court. So as far as America was concerned, no documents, no case.

I must say the decision to quit brought with it a sense of overwhelming relief. Of course we wouldn't have any news of George until we met in London, but we weren't anxious about him. We reckoned the three of us had probably made around $90,000. We would have to pay $10,000 to our three police department protectors in New York, our expenses would be about another $10,000, so we'd have around $23,000 each. Over the hors d'oeuvres we toasted our success, over the entrée we planned how we would spend our money, over the dessert we both agreed it wasn't enough, and over the coffee we committed each other to think of some scheme to raise more revenue as soon as we got safely to London.

Before we went separately to the railway station I took Mac's tall hat to the hatter's and left it to be ironed. This of course was simply to get rid of it and leave no trace behind. I bought a ticket for Belgium and Mac bought one for Amsterdam, both taking us through Cologne. We did not speak to each other and travelled separately. At Cologne we both got off the train and went to the cathedral. There we exchanged tickets and decided to catch the train from Cologne to Ostend, where we would take the boat for Dover. At the station in Cologne I bought a ticket to London via Ostend; Mac would buy his ticket for London when he arrived in Ostend. All these precautions may seem complicated, but you must remember that if the Germans had discovered any of our frauds they could have easily arrested Mac while he was still on the Continent, but there was no way in which they would be able to associate me with him so long as we were not seen together, and did not have similar tickets for similar destinations.

As it proved, we were not discovered. We reached Dover without mishap and in London we went straight to our arranged rendezvous, the Terminus Hotel at London Bridge. That evening I opened my door in response to a loud knock, and he walked in, wreathed in smiles.

After George delivered his report, which I communicated to you earlier, he opened a bottle of champagne and said: "I've been thinking. We could all do with a holiday in the sun after what we've been through. Why don't we all go off to Italy for a couple of weeks?"

Terrific idea! We all drank to it. I went to bed that night with visual scenes of Pompeii, Vesuvius, and Roman senators in purple togas swirling though my sleep-crushed mind. But before the very next day was out we had already pushed aside all our holiday plans and were hard at work plotting something bigger and more exciting than I had ever dreamed of.

5

I PLAY THE AMERICAN SILVER KING

With all the speed and complexity of the previous five days' work, our accounts were in something of a muddle, so we decided to throw all our money and gold on the table and do a reckoning up. The main item to be deducted was $10,000 for Jimmy Irving and Co of New York. Our expenses and other gifts and presents earmarked for America, which we agreed should come out of the common pool, accounted for nearly $20,000. The remainder we split three ways.

This seemed the fairest way of doing things. It also had the advantage of drawing us all closer together and consequently increasing our faith in each other, as well as reducing chances of any dispute. Brimming with happiness with our lot, we went out on the town, determined to behave like three real American tourists in London.

It was towards the end of that unforgettable day, as I have already recounted, that we strolled down Lombard Street after our visit to Hampton Court, and discovered there in front of us the Bank of England. Next day, in the throne room of Windsor Castle, the die was cast.

"We need another hundred thousand pounds each," I said simply, over dinner that night. "The only place where I can think of getting that kind of money is the Bank of England."

"The thing to remember about the Bank is this," said Mac. "Any system of finance unchanged in detail for a century must in the very nature of things be highly vulnerable. Especially when that system has become an article of faith not only with the Bank's officials, but with everyone else in England."

"Agreed," said George. "But against their vulnerability you must see that we start without any knowledge whatsoever of the Bank's inner workings. We're strangers in London, staying here under assumed names, without business of any kind, unable to give any references and unable to stand much investigation. We've got to improve on that for starters!"

Although from the outset we were confident we could crack the Bank – confidence is the supreme asset of the confidence trickster – George was right. We hadn't yet devised any plan. Because we now had some fifty thousand dollars between us, we wanted to avoid the obvious risks of forged letters of credit. As dinner progressed we gradually evolved the skeleton of an idea. In some way or other one of us would get an introduction to the Bank and use all our collective wealth to establish a credit there. The important first move was to open an account, which, because of the Bank's exclusivity was no easy thing to do; after that we would decide what use to put it to.

As I had taken a minor role in the previous business, I volunteered to be the front man in this one. I told my two friends they could go off on holiday to the Continent if they liked while I stayed in London and set the wheels in motion. They took me at my word and left for Spain next day.

I decided I would use only $20,000 to start the thing with, since it wasn't necessary to risk everything at once. I thought perhaps I should find some solicitor who kept an account at the Bank of England and hire him for a retaining fee of £100 as my legal adviser, telling him some fairy tale about establishing a London branch of my business. I would be lucky if so soon in our relationship he introduced me to the Bank as a prospective client, and even if he did that he might advise them later, with all the caution of a lawman, that I was a stranger to him. Indeed, even if I were introduced I would need a reference. Then I told myself that any solicitor with an account at the Bank of England would be regarded as "highly respectable", a term which in England I had come to associate with mediocrity. Finally I discarded the idea of a solicitor, and decided instead to find some old-established shopkeeper who kept an account at the Bank, and somehow to get an introduction through him.

At 2 p.m. on the day my friends left for the Continent I stationed myself near the Bank to watch depositors coming out. As a student of banks, I knew that when depositors take money to a bank four out of five of them come out examining their paying-in book. That afternoon I followed several of them. Of these I selected three. One was an optician and electrician, an old-established firm doing a large business. The second was an East India importing house. The third was Green and Son, tailors.

I had already decided I would need a new persona for this job, so now I resolved to play the role of the American Silver King. I had brought with me from America a Western hat, and planting it firmly on my head I set off. I went to the optician and bought an expensive opera glass, asking him in an exaggerated Kentucky drawl to engrave it with the words "To Lady Mary, from her friend," and paying for it with a £100 note. Then I went to the East India firm, bought an expensive white silk shawl and a dressing-gown fit for a prince, and looked at a camel-hair shawl for a hundred guineas.

The way I was treated would have done justice to visiting royalty. The English have absurd ideas about American Silver Kings. They take the stage article for the genuine, and they seem convinced that the Western pavements of America are thick with super-rich dudes with ploughboy drawls, marching around with thousand-dollar rolls in their pockets, which they throw out to bootblacks and bartenders.

Thoroughly enjoying the role, I drove in my hired brougham up to Green and Son and went in smoking a cigar, with my big hat pulled well down over my eyes. As soon as I saw the elder Green I knew I had my man. The family firm had had their account with the Bank of England for nearly a century and were extremely wealthy, although in the fashion of the English they stuck steadily to business. Their product was high fashion but, like many an historic English tailoring firm they charged more for their reputation than for the fit of their garments.

As I surveyed their merchandise a tailor and his assistant flew to serve me. Paying no attention, I started a slow march around the establishment, examining everything, with them both at my heels. When I had done a circuit I stopped and, pointing first at one roll of cloth and then another, said: "One suit from this, three suits from that, two from that, a topcoat from that, another from that, another suit from that, one from that. Now show me some dressing-gowns." The first they showed me was 20 guineas. I gave it half a glance and said it would do.

The tailor and his assistant were hitting the panic button. One measured, falling over his tape, the other wrote down the measurements, his hand trembling, both of them anxious not to lose this Yankee sheep that Providence had led astray into their shop. My name and address? Of course, my name and address. I gave them the first name that came into my head. I was F. A. Warren, Golden Cross Hotel. It was a name which in the fullness of time would be known all over England but at that moment, for fear I might forget it, I wrote it down myself and put it in my waistcoat pocket. They bowed me out, greatly impressed with my apparent wealth and with my big hat, confident they had hooked a fortune in a genuine American Silver King. I got in the brougham and drove directly to the Golden Cross Hotel, where I registered in the name of F. A. Warren. I kept the room for a whole year but never slept there. It was the only address the Bank of England ever had of its most talked-about customer.

Green and Co.! I had made up my mind to settle for them. At the end of the week I called and tried on my clothes.

"When you are ready to deliver, let me know and I will leave the cash with the hotel people," I drawled. I let another ten days go by before driving up to the shop again. Now, ostentatiously, I waited in my carriage as the head of the firm came out, bowing nearly to the pavement.

"Ah, Mr. Warren. Good morning, sir."

"Good morning to you, Mr. Green. I'm in a hurry and I need some more clothes. Perhaps you would be good enough to duplicate my original order."

His mouth dropped, and before he could find words to put into it I drove off.

Another week went by. I called at Green's to try on my new clothes, and this time I had the full undivided attention of the senior Green. When everything was satisfactory I said: "I'm off to Ireland tomorrow for a few days' shooting with Lord Clancarty. I'll send down a portmanteau for these clothes and call for it on my way from the hotel to the station."

I went out and bought the most expensive trunk I could find and sent it round to the tailor. When the day came for me to call I provided myself with six £500 banknotes, five £100s, and about fifty fivers to go at the bottom of the roll. I had a large trunk put on my cab and drove to the tailor's, where Mr. Green was waiting obsequiously for me.

"How much do I owe you?" I asked him. I didn't wait for his answer. I took out the bankroll and gave him a £500 note, making sure he saw the £500s under it. As my brand-new portmanteau was being hoisted on to the cab I said diffidently: "I have a bit of a problem, Mr. Green. I've got more money than I care to carry loose on me to Ireland. I wonder if I might leave it in your safe keeping?"

"Certainly, sir," replied the rich tailor, somewhat taken aback. As I was pulling out my bankroll he asked: "How much is it?"

"Only four thousand, it might be five thousand."

"Oh, sir, I would be afraid to take charge of so much. Let me introduce you to my bank."

He ran for his hat, took me to the Bank of England and, calling for one of the sub-managers, introduced me as an American gentleman, Mr. F. A. Warren, who wanted to open an account. A cheque-book and paying-in book were brought, and the signature book was put in front of me for my autograph.

"I wonder if you would mind signing your full name, sir," the sub-manager said.

I picked up a pen, dipped it in the inkwell, and thought of two appropriate Christian names. Thus the soon to be famous F. A. Warren was christened Frederick Albert. Thus too the Bank made its first error; the sub-manager, no doubt impressed by the worthy Mr. Green and by the five thousand dollars cash I was paying in, failed to ask for the written reference which the rules obliged him to demand. It was an error which was to cost the Bank dearly.

When Mac and George returned to England from their holiday and heard I was already an account-holder they jumped for joy. It even occurred to us as we talked together excitedly at my hotel, the Grosvenor at Victoria Station, that with this kind of start we could actually go straight. Mac and George could launch a business in London as brokers and promoters of stock companies. I could place £10,000 of our money in my Bank of England account and they would begin to buy and sell stock, keeping the money constantly on the move. The impressionable English would never cease hearing about "our Mr. F. A. Warren of the Bank of England," and business would surely boom. I think it would have worked. The two insurmountable problems were that we were looking for a short cut to wealth, and we wanted to get home again.

For several days we mulled over plans. They all centred on borrowing from day to day large sums on Mac's carefully forged securities. The downside from our point of view was that the Bank as a matter of course would keep these documents, which at any future time could be used in a criminal court against us. As preliminary reconnoitring I made several visits to the Bank, depositing and drawing out different sums. I had talks with the sub-manager and, on various pretexts to get information, I got acquainted with bankers and money men in the city. All these moves when we talked together about them led the three of us increasingly to believe that the boasted impregnability of the Bank of England was entirely imaginary.

Even so we reckoned we would need six months of preparation. The more we talked the blacker the word forgery seemed to become. Then as so often happens when one talks about an idea for too long we suddenly decided to give up the whole thing.

"Listen," said Mac, "there's no point in tackling something that's going to take that long to set up when we can make an easy killing somewhere else. There's no cable from Rio de Janeiro to Europe, and it takes forty days to send a letter from there and get a reply. Let's go to South America!"

"With that kind of time delay we could pull exactly the same trick we pulled in France and Germany," George said. He had always had one or two lingering doubts about the Bank of England job. "You could leave your account at the Bank. If we hit the jackpot in South America we can let the Bank keep the million or two we want from them. If we hit trouble, we'll come back and use your account to do the London job."

I didn't need much convincing. In no time at all we had forged documents giving us credit on the London and Westminster Bank. But before we left I needed to make one more visit to the Bank of England. I had a balance there of £2,335, and we had decided we needed all our capital ready at hand. Mac and George were both a bit sceptical about my relations with the Bank; they were sure F. A. Warren was regarded as a suspicious customer.

"All right," I said. "They've broken one rule for me. I'll show you that they'll break another one too."

I told the sub-manager that I was shortly leaving for St. Petersburg, then going on to Southern Russia to inspect some railway contracting work I was doing there, and therefore proposed to withdraw my account.

"Oh, please don't do that, Mr. Warren," he begged. "It really is a great pleasure for the Bank to have you as a customer. We very much admire your flair for business. Surely it would be convenient for you to keep an open account in London?"

"Well," I said, glancing at my passbook. "I see I have £2,335 to my credit. I will if you like leave the odd £35 with you."

"Of course," he said at once. "That will be quite in order."

I had him! He knew, and I knew he knew, that the Bank's rules required a minimum balance of £300. Had he said, "No, you must leave £300, as our rules require," I would have said, "All right," and made it £500. As it was, I drew out the £2,300 at once, and my balance at the Bank stood at £35 for all the weeks I was playing the pirate on the Spanish Main.

Stowing most of our baggage in London we took the train to Liverpool and bought tickets for the liner *Lusitania,* which was to end up many years later at the bottom of the ocean.* Mac bought his tickets in the name of Gregory Morrison and carried letters of intro-

* She was torpedoed off Cork by a German submarine on 7th May, 1915.

duction which he had forged himself to Maua and Co, who had branches in all the principal cities on South America's east and west coasts, including Montevideo, Buenos Aires, Lima, Valparaiso, Callao, and Rio.

From the moment of our arrival in Liverpool we were outwardly strangers and during the voyage no one suspected we were anything else. The saloon passengers were a merry lot. There was only one lady, the wife of a British army captain, who was going for a few months hunting on the Argentinean pampas; she was accompanied by a vast number of dogs and an assortment of guns. There was a Royal Navy chaplain, a huge man aged about 28, who drank champagne all day and constantly invited everyone who passed to "toss me for a bottle of fizz, old fellow". Among the 25 young male passengers was a party of 15 British civil engineers, who were going under the leadership of a Swedish colonel to survey, for the Brazilian Government, a railway line across the southern part of Brazil from the Atlantic to the Pacific; with that daunting prospect ahead of them they were determined to extract the last ounce of fun out of the 22-day voyage.

We of course joined in the frolics, but we also had plenty of time for discussion – too much, as it turned out; we might have done better if we had had less time to think about things. Our plan was that once again I should be
the background man, standing by if any of the other two came to grief. Mac was to present himself to Maua and Co. in Rio and to draw at least £10,000 within 24 hours, so as to make sure of our expenses.

A day or two before we were due to go aboard ship for our next port he was to arrange for a larger sum, £20,000 or £30,000. The moment he had this money George was to go to the Bank of London and Rio de Janeiro and secure as much as he thought it safe to ask for, £5,000 or £10,000. This would be paid in Brazilian paper money, which I was to exchange for sovereigns.

I was then to buy a ticket for the steamer going south, take the gold on board and stow it in my stateroom. At the last moment, in the bustle and confusion of sailing, Mac and George were to slip into my stateroom, hide, and sail with the steamer. Once out of harbour they were to see the purser, explain that they had arranged with a friend to buy tickets, but he hadn't showed up so they would have had to pay a second time. We thought this subterfuge with Mac and George was absolutely necessary, for if anything was discovered while they were on land the police would be everywhere and they would never be able to board a steamer legally – they simply had to vanish into thin air.

A few hours after our arrival in Rio Mac called at Maua's. He told the manager, Ramon Plomero, that his letters of credit ran from £5,000 to £20,000 each, and that he should want £10,000 the next day. Would they have it ready? I meanwhile called at the three largest money brokers and arranged to buy gold within 24 hours.

The next day Mac went back to Maua's while George and I posted ourselves outside. In ten minutes Mac reappeared with a square bundle under his arm. He smiled as he passed us, and turning a corner went into a cafe, where we joined him.

"There you are," he said, putting the bundle on the table. "It contains £10,000 in Brazilian notes. It was easy. I could have had £100,000 if I'd asked for it."

Picking up the bundle and a leather bag I'd bought for the purpose, I went out, hired a porter, and went swiftly round the brokers, buying sovereigns for the whole £10,000. By the time I was finished my porter was carrying 168 lbs in weight. He put it on his head and followed me to my hotel.

Now Mac had to go for the big sum, and from his previous visit to Maua's it looked pretty simple. He was ushered into Senhor Plomero's office and asked to sit down.

"I wonder if I might just take another look at the letter of credit on which we endorsed your £10,000 the other day," the manager began easily.

Mac was a man of iron nerve, but that was a request that would have blown the *Lusitania* off course.

"Certainly," he said, composing himself and producing the letter.

Plomero studied it for a moment. "This is most singular," he said. "There is only the name of Mr. Bradshaw, the manager of the London and Westminster Bank in London, on this letter. But the name of the sub-manager, J. P. Shipp, should be on it as well. I know this because I recall that some time ago we were notified by the London bank that all letters issued by them would bear two signatures."

Mac swallowed. "All I can suggest is that I check with my other letters of credit, which I've left in my hotel, and come back to you," he said. "I'm sure they carry both signatures." He was of course quite sure that they didn't, but Plomero acquiesced.

Posted outside Maua's, we knew something was wrong just by the look on his face as he came out. We followed him at a distance back to his hotel, and inside he told us what had happened.

Mac and I were convinced that the game was up, and began to plan our escape. But George, usually so circumspect, wanted to take up the challenge.

"The manager's only seen one credit," he argued. "We've got to put this fellow Shipp's name on the others. You've got it on the genuine draft which you copied from."

"It took me a month to write those letters of credit," Mac said. "It'll take me another month to alter them."

"Let's see what you can do after a treble brandy," replied George.

We gave him a drink, put the genuine signature in front of him, and the forged letters, and set him to work. I can remember how he did it to this day. The signatures were not well written, but given all the circumstances they were wonderful. When he had finished George said:

"Listen, Mac, I know how you feel, but you've got to take them back to Maua's right away. Tell them that the other letters were all right, that the second signature was omitted only from the one you presented the other day. If there's a problem, rely on us to get you out of it somehow. Just keep cool. The manager will never believe you could have forged the signatures in so short a time. If there's any hesitation, tell him you'll transfer your business to the English Bank of Rio at once."

He was a brave fellow, our Mac. He started out on the decisive errand, followed by us at a safe distance. Afterwards he told us that Plomero was clearly surprised when shown the other letters with both signatures, and transferred the endorsement from the letter with one signature to one of those that had two.

We decided to relax for a few days after that and see something of the country. One day we took an early train and stopped off at a small hamlet by a stream about thirty miles from Rio, beyond the mountain range that hems in the city. Slavery was still the law of the land, and the poor slave was everywhere in evidence. We found some saddle mules and started off into the wilds. The hills were covered with coffee bushes filled with red fruit, about the size of a cherry, each containing two kernels. The coffee was picked into large flat baskets by slaves and when the baskets were filled they carried them on their heads to the drying grounds.

The roads were lined with orange trees loaded with luscious fruit, to which we helped ourselves. After a long ride we came to a coffee plantation, where the slaves were just on their way to dinner. Thirty or forty slaves of both sexes and all ages sat down on the grass and ate a blackish stew out of metal dishes with their fingers. They stared in stupid wonder as we three horsemen rode out of the forest, until one went to fetch the overseer. Presently a white man appeared, and in response to Mac's *"Lei parlate Italiano?"* came the smiling answer, *"Si, Signor."*

The overseer gave us a guided tour of the place, explaining all the processes of preparing coffee for the market. In one corner of a large, unpainted building was what he called the infirmary, and a comfortless-looking place it was too. He said there was no doctor on the plantation, and he dealt out medicines to the sick slaves himself. Did he ever find his medicine unequal to the sickness, we asked him over coffee? Occasionally yes, he replied, and that was most unfortunate, because while slaves were certainly replaceable, new ones involved a small capital outlay. On our way back to Rio Mac regaled us with his views on the avariciousness of the human race, and speculated on what the coffee-plantation overseers would have to say for themselves about their outrageous exploitation of their fellow human beings when they were called to meet their Maker.

The next day was Friday. The mail steamer Ebro was to leave Rio the following Wednesday for Liverpool, carrying with it the draft for £10,000 on the London and Westminster Bank, along with a letter from the Rio bank, stating that they had cashed Mr. Gregory Morrison's draft upon the letter issued by them.

Twenty-two or three days after the steamer left Rio the London bank would know about the fraud, but with no way to bridge the intervening 8,000 miles except by steam, we calculated we had forty-four more days to gather in our harvest. On the same Wednesday that the *Ebro* set sail for Liverpool we planned to book passage with our 160 lbs. of sovereigns on the *Chimborazo,* heading for the River Plate and the west coast. So it was agreed that on Monday, 48 hours before we sailed from Rio, Mac should go to Maua's and arrange to cash his letters for twenty or thirty thousand pounds, and go the next day, Tuesday, for the money. As soon as he left the bank and told us all was well, another of us was to call at the Bank of London and Rio, and at the River Plate Bank, present his letters of introduction, and ask in each bank to have the five or ten thousands pounds ready by 11 a.m. next day. This would give me time to exchange the Brazilian banknotes for sovereigns, to buy my ticket on the *Chimborazo,* secure my stateroom and get the gold to the steamer.

More important than any of these things, it would give me time to get my passport stamped by the Brazilian police, for it is a law of the country that no one may leave it, native or visiting foreigner, without having his passport so stamped.

On Monday morning we went into a public park for our last discussion on our plan. At 10.45 Mac jumped up from the park seat exclaiming, "Time to be off!" We followed him, posted ourselves outside Maua's, and waited. It was as well that we had no knowledge until afterwards of what was happening inside.

Plomero received Mac cordially again and chatted pleasantly over coffee. Then Mac said: "I shall require £20,000 tomorrow, could you have it ready?"

"Well, Mr. Morrison," Plomero replied, "I don't really require any more exchange on London. But I'll send out for my broker, who will sell your bills on the exchange. Then I will endorse the bills of exchange and endorse the amounts on your letters of credit."

Mac didn't like that very much, but he had to agree. Accordingly, the broker, a Senhor Meyers, was summoned by the firm's clerk.

"This is Mr. Gregory Morrison," Plomero said. "I'd like you to see exchange for £20,000 on his credit, which I will endorse."

"Delighted to help you, Mr. Morrison," said Meyers. "May I see your letters?"

Mac put his hand into his breast pocket, pulled out the little morocco leather case in which he had put his two letters, each for £20,000, and handed case and contents to Meyers. The broker ran his sharp eyes down one of them, reading right through the body of the letter, until he came to the "note", which read:

"All sums drawn against this credit please endorce on the back, and notify the London and Westminster Bank at once."

The broker raised his eyes from the letter and fixed Mac with a long, hard stare.

"How very strange, sir," he said, "they have misspelled the word endorse. Surely the clerks in London banks know how to spell their own language?"

6

FAST EXIT FROM SOUTH AMERICA

You may depend upon it that Maua's of Rio had never met a customer as cool as Mr. Gregory Morrison. Airily he brushed aside Meyers' thunderbolt.

"I should think it's just a slip of the pen," he said. "I imagine it's very easy for a clerk to allow his attention to wander if he is writing all day at his desk."

"You are absolutely right, Mr. Morrison," Senhor Plomero said, in a way which suggested he had irritating first-hand knowledge of similar instances.

This intervention on his side gave Mac the split second he needed to think.

"You know, I'm not sure that I care to have my bills sold on the exchange," he said. "The simple solution is for me to go round to the London and Rio Bank, and the River Plate Bank. They probably want exchange, and I'm sure they would let me have the money I require."

Meyers said sharply: "Do you have letters to those banks?"

For answer Mac produced two letters, one to each bank, each bearing the expertly forged stamp of their establishment. This was a masterstroke. That such letters existed was due entirely to our foresight that an emergency might occur. Mac had no doubt that his dramatic production of the letters lulled the suspicions that were gathering in Ramon Plomero's office.

"Of course I understand if you prefer to do that," Meyers said. "It will certainly be much easier for you."

The two Brazilians stood up and shook his hand warmly. Any time he wanted any help, he was to call in and see them. If they did not see him again before he returned to Europe they wished him a safe trip. Of one thing Mac was now certain: as soon as Plomero told Meyers that he had already parted with £10,000 the name of Gregory Morrison would be forwarded to the police.

When Mac came out of Maua's and told us what had happened, we knew we had to get out of the country as fast as we could.

Earlier I mentioned the Brazilian law that required everyone leaving the country to have their passport stamped by the police. When he is ready to leave the country a visitor must take his passport to police headquarters for the stamp and tell the officer which steamer he proposes to travel on. He then has to leave his passport with the agent from whom he buys his ticket. The agent checks with the police that the passenger is not wanted, and passes the passport on to the purser, who doesn't give it back to the passenger until the vessel is at sea. This is not an easy system to evade. At that time too there were no back doors to Brazil, for behind the coastal cities were thousands of miles of impenetrable forest, much of it unseen by man.

To make matters worse, here we were on Monday and the Chimborazo, going south, hadn't yet reached Rio; there was no hope that it would depart on schedule on Wednesday. The Ebro, however, going to Europe, was in the harbour taking on cargo and coal. Although the names in our American passports were the same as those on our letters, we had chemicals with us and writing inks with which Mac could alter the names and descriptions at will. Thus in the first move of the desperate plan we hatched, Mac changed George's name to George Wilson.

George went to police headquarters, got his passport stamped at once, then went to an agent and bought a ticket for Liverpool on the Ebro. Next he took a boat and went out to the steamer, carrying with him two bags of oranges which he stowed away under the bottom berths.

We needed the agent to get really well acquainted with "George Wilson's" face and appearance, so if the question were asked: "Who is this Wilson?" the police would know by the description that it was not the man they were looking for. For the next forty-eight hours, therefore, George badgered the agent until the poor fellow was quite exhausted. At one time George would want to know if he couldn't get some reduction on the fare, or if the *Ebro* were seaworthy, or if the engines might break down, and so on, until the agent not only got to know Mr. Wilson but fervently wished him at the bottom of the sea.

Mac, meanwhile, decided it was absolutely essential that he should put in one more appearance at Maua's. He called in and casually told Ramon Plomero that he was starting next morning for Sao Romao, a town in the interior, and would be there for a week. It was, Mac afterwards remembered, an extraordinary conversation, because he was sure Plomero had informed the police about him, and equally sure that both the manager and the police were relying on the passport system to prevent him leaving the country. Plomero was as cordial as ever, and wished him a safe journey. Then Mac returned to his hotel, paid his bill, and mentioned that he was leaving by the four o'clock train next morning for Sao Paulo.

Mac had two trunks and other impedimenta befitting a man of his importance, so he needed a carriage to the station, nearly a mile away. It would be unsafe to use the hotel carriage; he therefore told the hotel a friend would call for him.

It was still two hours to sunset, so in order to find out whether Mac was being tailed, we told him to saunter out and walk about the streets until dark, while we kept him in view, then return to the hotel and be ready when

George would call for him at 3 a.m. We soon saw what we feared. As soon as Mac left his hotel it was clear that a man was following him, and even tracked him back into his hotel.

It was just as well that George and I decided not to tell Mac what we had seen, for at 3 a.m. Mac appeared with his luggage and said to us: "Do you mind if we give someone a lift? I met this chap in the hotel last night and it so happens he's going to Sao Romao by our train too. I had a long chat with him last night, and he seems a good fellow."

I hadn't the slightest doubt who the mysterious stranger was. Mac must have seen the look of disapproval that flashed across my face because he added: "Well, you know, he said he'd never be able to get a carriage at this time of the morning. He's waiting upstairs now."

"Forget it, Mac," I said. "Go and tell him we're loaded down with luggage and we haven't got an inch more room."

Fortunately, he was able to do this without much fuss. On the way to the station I said: "We think this guy is following you. If he is, somehow he's going to find some transport to get to the station and catch your train. Stand near the ticket office until he arrives. If he buys a first-class ticket, you buy a second, and vice-versa."

"Don't worry," Mac said. "I'll give him the slip."

He did, too. He waited in the station shadows until the stranger came puffing in and bought a ticket. The man watched Mac get into a compartment just as the train started, and then got into another himself. What he didn't see was Mac opening the door on the other side of the compartment and dropping out on to the track as the train was moving. The stranger was set for a long ride; there was only one train a day each way, and the return one wouldn't get him back into Rio until the end of the day.

Within a couple of minutes Mac was back in our carriage. For the benefit of the coachman we then had a dialogue somewhat like this:

"Too bad! " Mac groaned. "Our friends weren't on the train. What are we going to do now?"

"We'll have to go back to the hotel and wait for the afternoon train," I replied.

"But I've already paid my bill there."

"You'll have to kill the day in Rio and then meet me at the station. I'll look after the luggage."

The idea was that in the event of the police recovering the trail, any information they got from the driver would hopefully cause enough confusion and delay to enable us to get out of Rio.

I told the coachman to drive me into the city. I dropped off Mac first, then George, and drove on a little way. It was still dark, but after a while I saw a tavern and restaurant combined. Here I arranged with the owner to look after our baggage, and dismissed the driver. Then I walked to another tavern where we had arranged that George should hire a room. George and Mac were already waiting there for me.

We now had Mac hidden away, and felt reasonably safe for the moment. At daybreak George left to take Mac's baggage off to the *Ebro*. The ship was anchored out in the bay, with strings of barges loaded with sacks of coffee alongside. She was, George was told, sailing sharp at noon on Wednesday, the next day. For the remainder of that Tuesday George and I came and went, arranging things for our escape, while poor old Mac had to sit there holed up in the room and miserable with the inactivity.

Near our tavern was a boat stand, from which George arranged for us to have a boat to take us out to the *Ebro*. We knew that by midnight there would be quite a number of early arriving passengers already on the ship, and that the bay would be filled with all the bustle and confusion that happens when a ship is receiving and stowing cargo.

At 9 p.m. I left to go back to my hotel and get the remainder of the sovereigns not yet on board, about £4,000 worth. I was back with the gold within an hour. Now we set out for the boat stand and soon had two rowers pulling us towards the *Ebro*. Three or four small boats were fastened to the companion ladder, so our arrival attracted no attention. We slipped along the deck and into George's stateroom. Then, promising to return on board at 8 a.m. with their breakfast, I said goodbye to my friends.

That night I slept soundly ashore, got up early, break-fasted, and returned across the bay with George and Mac's breakfast. Before I went on board I gave my two boatmen five gold sovereigns.

"Listen to me carefully," I said, in a mixture of Spanish, English and Italian. "I will give you another ten gold sovereigns each if you obey my orders. I want you to stay alongside this steamer until it begins to move out of harbour. Stay on the blind side of the ship beneath the companion-way, and as the ship pulls away I will arrive with a friend; you can then row us back to shore."

I left the two fellows goggling at the gold I'd given them, and chanting, *"Si, senhor, si, si!"* as I went up the companion-way with the breakfast tray. While Mac and George fell on the food I went out on deck to scrutinise the small boats coming and going from our ship.

I soon saw what I was expecting. First a boatload of policemen, and then following them a smaller boat con-taining the man described by Mac as Ramon Plomero, with another civilian whom I supposed was a bank offi-cial. None of these people knew me, of course, so I was able to watch them take up their positions on the deck, from which they began to scrutinise every small boat arriving. It was a job to keep any observer busy, for there were now about 60 small boats constantly buzzing around the *Ebro*, most of them containing salesmen try-ing to interest the passengers in everything from oranges and bananas to monkeys, snakes and parrots.

Soon after 10 a.m. the enemy was joined by another boat containing the ticket agent, and I could see they were contemplating some action. I slipped down to George's stateroom and reported that a search party would come by probably within an hour; I would try to give them a few minutes warning before it arrived. Back on deck I saw the agent now had a manifest of passengers and an enormous heap of passports. After some chat with the police the passports were sent back to the purser. With the manifest in hand the agent, the police and Plomero now began a search of the ship while I hurried below to report.

Divesting himself of his jacket, waistcoat and dignity, Mac crept under the lower berth. We put a bag of oranges in front of him, dispersing them so that they filled the whole space.

Then we opened the door as wide as possible, uncorked a bottle of iced claret, and filled two glasses. With my glass in my hand I sat on the edge of the lower berth, smoking and swinging my feet. George sat on a stool, facing the door but not obstructing the view. Soon the search party arrived, headed by the ticket agent. When he saw George, whom he knew only too well, he said "How do you do, Mr. Wilson?" and passed on without looking in. Plomero and the police followed, glanced equally casually at the two of us and passed on. By 11.30 they were all back up on the upper deck, evidently satisfied that Gregory Morrison wasn't on board, and watching the new arrivals. We dragged poor Mac, half roasted by the stifling heat, from out behind the oranges, and at once he polished off the bottle of iced claret.

At ten to twelve the bell was rung and all those on board who were not sailing with the ship were asked to leave. The police and Plomero went with them in their respective boats. We listened as the steam winch lifted the anchor, the screw began to revolve and the *Ebro* forged slowly ahead. That was the signal for George and

I to move like lightning. We ran to the upper deck and down the steps on the blind side of the ship and almost fell into my boat. When they saw the glint of ten more gold sovereigns the two boatmen couldn't pull hard enough for the shore; I actually had to slow them down lest they caught up with the police boat.

Mac was free at last, with George's passport and George's ticket. We had his passport, which we altered to fit George's description, and several days later we sailed on the *Chimborazo* to Montevideo. As the steamer slipped out of Rio we looked back on the Sugar Loaf and on the ruin of our buccaneering expedition on the Spanish Main – a failure except for the £10,000 we had captured.

Any slim hopes of restarting our enterprise were dashed when we arrived at Montevideo. Together with all the other passengers for the city, we were put in quarantine for ten days on a vile little island called the Isle of Flowers. The mails, however, were fumigated and sent through. When our quarantine was over we were allowed into the city, and soon heard that a sinister story had reached there from Rio about an American businessman named Gregory Morrison. So we destroyed all our financial documents, made a quick visit to Buenos Aires, and then embarked on a French ship for Marseilles. The day after our arrival we were in Paris, where we met up with Mac at the Hotel Meurice in the Rue Rivoli.

Paris – even that somewhat humiliated Paris of 1872 – was a good city for thinking. And we began to think. Something in the air there must have lightened our thoughts, for all three of us talked of going straight. We had a collective obsession with Colorado, and now we planned to go there, start a bank and build a wheat elevator and stockyards. Fifty thousand dollars would start our bank, and $10,000, with some credit, would buy the elevator and yards. We had that sort of money, plus another $10,000 for cash flow.

Colorado was on our menu for lunch and dinner for days, and we were so determined to carry through this plan that we now decided to have a last tourist fling in Europe. We visited the battlefields of the recent war with Germany, went to Vienna, dined by the Danube, and from there to Wiesbaden, which I suppose, with the benefit of hindsight, was our undoing. For at Wiesbaden we drifted into the casino and watched such vast sums changing hands that they put our modest capital into perspective, and by the end of our first evening there we were all agreed that we simply didn't have enough capital to start up in business in the States.

"We have too many skills to give up now," Mac reasoned. "We could make a lot more money in Europe."

"We ought to try to double our capital, even treble it, at least before we quit," George said.

And I agreed. "Well, gentlemen, if we need some starting-point, we have here among us one Frederick Albert Warren, a customer of the Bank of England, whose uncounted millions he is anxious to sample."

Our minds were made up. It was June when we decided to set out for London, to start work on a plan to rouse the Old Lady of Threadneedle Street from a century-long slumber spent in dreaming of her impregnability. When I look back now, forty years later, at the way Colorado has developed, I don't know whether to laugh or cry.

Before we left Wiesbaden for London Mac sat down and wrote a letter to the Bank of England in French, signing it H. V. Fischer. The name was important because in Frankfurt there were several banking firms named Fischer, and the manager of the Bank of England would therefore suppose that his correspondent was one of these Fischer bankers. In the letter Mr. Fischer said his distinguished customer, Mr. F. A. Warren, had written to him from St. Petersburg asking him to transfer to his Bank of England account the small balance remaining to his credit on Fischer's books; therefore he had the honour to enclose bills on London for £13,500, payable to the order of the manager, said sum to be placed to the credit of Mr. F. A. Warren.

I took this letter to Frankfurt, and having bought the necessary bills of exchange on London, enclosed them and posted the letter. Several days later I received a letter at Frankfurt from the Bank of England manager, Mr. P. M. Francis, acknowledging receipt of the drafts and placing them to the credit of F. A. Warren. So I now had over $50,000 to my credit, and had been a depositor for five months.

George took up residence at a private house in the West End, and Mac and I booked in at the Grosvenor Hotel. I had, as you know, stayed there before. Its advantage was that it was "highly respectable", which in the English of England meant that it was exclusive, and therefore a fit dwelling-place for the rich and aristocratic. Unfortunately, the cuisine was also highly respectable – that is, for dinner one could eat roast, either beef or mutton, vegetables limited to turnips, cauliflowers, cabbage and potatoes, and for dessert, the famous apple pie of England, which is more deadly even than the mince pie of America. We solved this problem by sleeping at the Grosvenor and eating at a restaurant nearby. We also took out a long lease on a room in a private house in Finsbury, which was our "safe place" for consultations and escape, if escape should ever need to be contemplated.

So far since our return to London I hadn't visited the Bank, nor did I yet intend to. I arranged through a courier to send some more funds, some of the sovereigns Mac had brought back from Brazil, to be credited to my account, raising my balance to $67,000, before setting out for Paris, the first of many trips I was going to make to the Continent. At the Hotel Bristol, Place Vendome, a swell place where none but the great sirs o' the earth could afford to stay, I registered as F. A. Warren, London, and sent off a letter to Mr. Francis, manager of the Bank of England. It read:

Dear Sir,
I am a customer of the Bank, therefore I take the liberty of troubling you in the hope to have the benefit of your advice.

Will you kindly inform me what good 4 per cent stocks are to be had in the market, also if the Bank will transact the business for me?

> *I remain,*
> *Very truly yours,*
> *F. A. Warren.*

By return post came a letter which advised me to invest in India 4 per cents or London Gas. I wrote an immediate order to have the bank buy me £10,000 of India stock and sent a cheque for that amount, on his own bank, payable to the order of the manager. I received back the stock, instantly sold it, and replaced the money to my credit. Next day I sent off an order for £10,000 Gas stock, and repeated the operation until I had made the impression I wanted to make on the mind of the manager, which was that when I returned to London for my decisive interview and sent in my card he would at once recognise the name, F. A. Warren, as the multi-millionaire American who had been sending him £10,000 cheques from Paris.

All this, of course, necessitated my being in Paris for several weeks. Since I had nothing to do but enjoy myself, I determined to see every sight there was to see. I loved the history of France and every day set out in some new direction to absorb more of it. By night I was kept constantly amused by the antics of the rich American colony in Paris, eating huge amounts of expensive food and drinking even more expensive wines, none of which they understood, while they shouted their delight, in murderous French, about being in "Gay Paree" as they called it. I fear my fellow countrymen, despite being truly providence to the hotel keepers and restaurateurs, have made themselves the laughing stock of Paris.

And then it was back to London, to prepare myself for my interview with that great Sir of Sirs in the London financial world, the manager of the Bank of England.

7

ONE WAY TO CON A ROTHSCHILD

The overture to the grand opera was played out in my room at the Grosvenor, where Mac and I breakfasted together at 8 a.m. George joined us at 9 and we talked for an hour. Our chief concern was that although I had the account, and had used it vigorously to indicate that I was plainly very wealthy, they had no written reference on me, and therefore no idea who I was. But there was no point in dwelling on such shortcomings. At 10 we set out for the Bank. George and Mac remained outside while I went in and sent in my "F. A. Warren, Railway Contractor" card.

The interview was short.

"We're delighted to see you back in this country, Mr. Warren," the manager, Mr. Francis, said. "We will certainly do all in our power to accommodate you."

Evidently, just before my arrival he had refreshed his memory with a memorandum of my transactions over the past few weeks.

"I am, of course financing large sums," I said. "I shall need more discounts before the year is out."

"Have no fear, sir, I'm sure we will be able to assist you."

There was little more to say beyond the customary small talk, so we shook hands warmly and I left.

The following morning I went to the Continental Bank in Lombard Street, and bought sight exchange on Paris for 200,000 francs, paying for it by cheque on the Bank of England. I was given a note of identification to the Paris agent of the bank.

That night I left Victoria Station for Paris. At 10 next morning I had my money, and, going to the Place de la Bourse near the Exchange, I commissioned a broker who was a member of the Exchange to buy bills on London for £8,000. I told him he must buy bills drawn only on well-known banking houses. At 3 p.m. he had the bills ready and I paid him the amount, along with his commission.

Because some of these manoeuvres may seem complicated, I will explain for those readers not conversant with these financial transactions how they work. Imagine for a moment that John Russell, cotton broker in Savannah, ships a thousand bales of cotton to a firm in Manchester. The Manchester firm then authorises him to draw a bill of exchange on their firm, payable at some London bank at three or six months' time, for the value of the cotton.

Let us say the price is £10,000. Russell draws ten bills for £1,000 each, payable, say, at the Union Bank of London. He gives these bills to a money broker in Savannah, who sells them on the Exchange and gets for them whatever the rate of exchange may then be on London.

Meanwhile the president of the Georgia Central Railroad orders a thousand tons of steel rail in England for his railway, and to pay for them he orders a broker to buy for him bills on London to the amount of the cost of the steel rail. He buys the Russell bills, and these bills of exchange he sends in payment to the steel-rail manufacturers in England. Effectively the president of the Georgia Central pays Russell for his thousand bales of cotton, but has the bills of exchange. Instead of £10,000 in gold being freighted twice across the ocean, the ten pieces of paper cross only once. These ten bills of £1,000 each, drawn on the Union Bank of London at six months, are presented and accepted in due time and paid at maturity by the bank.

Instead of commercial notes or bills they are now known as acceptances, and are as good as a banknote. If the owner, no matter who he is, wants the money at once any bank will discount all or either for the face value less the interest. In every commercial centre of the world these accepted bills are being discounted by banks and moneyed corporations for enormous sums, but by no bank in the world in such huge amounts as by the Bank of England. At the time of which I am writing their daily discounts were running into millions.

It was this system I planned to use to relieve the Bank of some of those millions. Exactly how you will presently see.

I left Paris in the evening of my arrival there and after breakfasting next day with Mac I took my bills to the various banks on which they were drawn, and left them for acceptance. When I returned 24 hours later they bore across the face the magic words:

"London, Aug. 14, 1872.
Accepted for the Union Bank of London.
E. Barclay, Manager.
J. Wayland, Assistant Manager."

I hurried off to the Grosvenor, where Mac studied the bills intently. He had to know every loop of the handwriting, every mark in the printing, for it was to be his job to copy them exactly.

My job in the meantime was to present these and many more batches of genuine bills for discount at the Bank until the officials there were thoroughly accustomed to discounting for me. Meanwhile as fast as I got genuine acceptances and bills Mac would continue to make copies of them for future use, only leaving out the date until such time as we were ready to put them in for discount. The one big question mark over this plan was this. Was it the custom of the Bank of England in 1872 to send acceptances offered for discount to the acceptors for verification of signatures?

We simply didn't know the answer to that question.

Verification was then a matter of routine in America, but the success of our plan was built on the assumption that that was not the case in England. Our assumption turned out to be correct; indeed, had that elementary precaution been used by the Bank of England our scheme would have collapsed.

Taking my deposit book and the genuine bills I went to the Bank and left the bills for discount. When this was done the amount was placed to my credit. I drew £10,000 and that night left for the Continent, this time for Ostend and the train for Amsterdam. There I repeated the Paris operation, securing £10,000 in genuine bills. I returned to London, left them for acceptance, then Mac manufactured a lot of imitations and put them in store. The genuine bills were then discounted. Again and again I went to the Continent, repeating the operation, until at last my credit at the Bank was as firm as a rock, and we were ready to move in.

· But all these operations, simple as they might seem, took a good six months and cost us dearly. Our ordinary living expenses were not less than $25 a day for the three of us, while my travelling expenses were enormous. I probably travelled 10,000 miles across Europe, to Paris, Amsterdam, Frankfurt and Vienna, in my bill-buying expeditions, and of course for every bill I had to pay commission to the broker. At the end of six months I calculated that the total investment in our preparations was $15,000.

It is of course only fair to add that not all this money was spent on simple necessities. When submitting my expenses for the scrutiny of my two partners I had to confess that a man is not made of wood. On one trip to Frankfurt for instance, I was obliged to stay for two or three days, and bored with my own company I took the short trip over to Wiesbaden, where the famous casino beckoned me like a magnet.

On my first evening there I was standing at a table watching money ebbing and flowing in ocean-like quantities when I noticed an attractive, dark-eyed woman of about 40 sitting behind one of the biggest gamblers on the other side of the table. She was magnificently dressed, except that she wasn't wearing a single item of jewellery. Whenever this gambler won, he invariably passed a large token to the woman, who slipped it into a small evening handbag.

Presently the gambler gave up. He pushed back his chair, and taking his remaining chips disappeared towards the cash desk. To my great surprise the woman then seated herself behind another gambler on my side of the table, who as he won also passed a large chip back to her, which she immediately slipped into the handbag.

It seemed pretty clear to me that the woman was spending all her time around the tables, following the winners and getting *douceurs* from them. These were by no means small, and they seemed to be gifts pure and simple, given from mere goodness of heart or sheer prodigality, for there were enough beautiful women flocking around ready to smile on winners who, most of the casino frequenters knew, were ready to exchange their favours for cash.

After about half an hour the woman's second winner also decided to decamp from the table. The woman took his chair, and curious to see what would happen, I edged up behind her. She began betting modestly on the black, and three times in succession the red came up. I was close enough to see that on the fourth turn of the wheel she was staking her last gulden again on the black, and again the red came up.

The woman turned round in her chair, looked up at me, and said: "Sir, if you want to make some money now, please place a double Frederick on the red."

I placed the money on the red at once, and won. She then said: "Now put your winnings on the black." I did so, and black won. Placing her hand on the stake, she said: "Leave it, sir, black will win again." And it did.

She picked up the cash, $80, and handing me a double Frederick, said in a most bewitching manner: "Sir, please be generous and let me keep the rest."

"Certainly, madame," I replied. I watched her stake what I had given her, and in two more turns of the wheel it was gone. I smiled to myself, and before she could turn round I too was gone.

I went into the Musik Saal, sat at a table, ordered a bottle of wine, and listened to the music while watching the crowd coming and going. Presently the woman of the tables came in and seeing me alone asked if she might join me. We began to talk and she was quite fascinating. She seemed to have been everywhere in Europe and spoke half a dozen languages. We Americans, with our 3,000 miles of land mass between two great oceans, are continually fascinated by the cosmopolitan European, and I was about to order another bottle of Hochheimer (she had already helped me finish the first one) and ask her something of her origins when she said: "My first husband was a Hungarian Count, which of course makes me a Countess. But please don't stand on ceremony; call me by my first name, Elisabeth."

The Countess Elisabeth de Winzerode, none other, chased across Europe by my travelling detective friend for her clever fraud on the Van Tromp family! I could hardly tell her I knew about her, though I had a mind to, for I was already bewitched by her mature charm and I was beginning to recognise in her a kindred spirit. She had been the mistress, it seemed, of a dozen men – noblemen, diplomats, soldiers – but being an inveterate gambler she had wagered the cash, estates, diamonds, carriages, furs they had showered on her at the tables, at the Casino, or in the drawing-room games of the bon-ton in Paris or Petersburg, and lost the lot. She wasn't a bit unhappy about it, either.

"Money is to be enjoyed, Austin, not kept," she said, flashing her dark eyes. "You will see plenty of people at the spas trying to keep what they've got. Their bodies are broken and wrinkled, they have nothing to live for but their daily dose of pain and the perpetual fear of losing their money."

"But there is surely nothing dishonourable in devoting oneself to the business of making money, don't you think?"

"You don't make money, you only take it from other people."

How very true, I thought; this was exactly why I had come to Frankfurt.

We talked until long past midnight, putting the world to rights, as if we had known each other all our lives. The Casino began to empty out and thinking that we too should go, I accompanied her to where the carriages were waiting.

"My hotel is the Bellevue at Bieberich," she said. The town was about four miles away.

"I will tell the coachman to take you there."

"I hope you will accompany me. You Americans surely don't leave a lady to take herself home in a carriage at this hour of the night?"

Well, I thought, I've got nothing to lose except another hour, and the coachman would be in for a good night's work, for he could take me from Bieberich back to Frankfurt. So we jogged together side by side through the night, and long before we reached Bieberich her hand was in my hand and her lips were against mine and I had abandoned myself to the fortunes of the night.

The Bellevue was far from first-rate; in fact, it was hardly second-rate. Her room was plastered but unpapered, of average size and cheaply furnished. But the tattiness of the decor was more than compensated for by the Countess's magnificent, individualistic style of lovemaking. It did not take me long to understand why large *douceurs* were constantly being handed to her at the Casino, or why she had been the dazzling mistress of a dozen important men.

You must remember that I was still in my mid-twenties, not much conversant with bedroom arts, and here was a woman old enough to be my mother and still beautiful, with a still nubile body, as vagabond in spirit as I was but with ten lifetimes of experience, ready and willing to instruct me in the joys of being uninhibited. We made so much love that night that there wasn't even time enough for it, and we had to continue until the following afternoon.

I can never think of my carefree Countess without a quickening of my heart and a prayer of thankfulness that we met and gave ourselves to each other unforgettably for that night and the following day. After that my business, moving towards its heady climax, seemed almost boring.

By the autumn the Bank of England had been discounting comparatively large sums for me for weeks. Many thousand pounds of the genuine article discounted had matured, and been paid, and more thousands were still in the vaults, awaiting maturity, and would fall due, while our home-manufactured bills would be laid away in the vaults, there to remain for four or five months until due. Needless to say, a full month or two before that happened we would be on the other side of the world, I on some hacienda in Mexico, George and Mac in Florida, where we would hole up for a year or so until, by the skilful management of Jimmy Irving and the New York Police Department, the affair would have blown over and we could return to our native city.

We were now ready to strike. I was convinced everything was in order, but George, who as I have said was given much more to weighing up the risks than Mac and I, still wasn't satisfied.

"We need to make one more big test," he said. "One that will make such a big impression on the Bank manager that anything you do will pass completely unquestioned."

"A test?" Mac and I echoed together.

"I'll tell you what I've dreamed up. I think Austin should go to the Rothschilds in Paris and get a bill on

London drawn to the order of F. A. Warren direct. If he can do this the Bank will think he is a close business associate of the Rothschilds. As a minor consideration we could copy the Rothschild acceptance."

"Good God, George!" Mac exclaimed. "You know of course that Sir Anthony de Rothschild, the head of the London house whose name you are proposing to offer, is a director of the Bank of England?'

George nodded.

"What you're suggesting means he would have to pass his own paper for discount, paper bearing his name, manufactured by us."

Again George nodded.

"That's one terrific risk," Mac said softly. "It's a freaky idea, quite unnecessary and probably impossible."

"It'll cost us another £1,000 and a two-week delay," I added.

"Wait," said George, "I haven't finished yet. I think you should draw a bill at Rothschilds for £6,000. I don't mean six one-thousands – I mean one £6,000."

Mac and I looked at each other incredulously, then both of us burst out laughing. I should explain that any single bill of exchange is seldom drawn for more than £1,000, rarely for £2,000, and one of £6,000 is almost unheard of. If for instance a Bombay trader wanted exchange on London for £100,000, his broker would probably furnish him with a hundred bills for £1,000 each.

"I don't think it's impossible," George argued. "I think it could work, as everything else has worked so far. And if it works that well Austin will be one of the really big shots on the Bank's client list."

A single bill for £6,000 drawn on Rothschilds! It was a piece of arrogance neither Mac nor I would have dreamed of.

But George was nothing if not persuasive. So off I went again, buying 200,000 French francs at the exchange broker's in London, and steaming out of Victoria Station for the Continent on the start of a journey I will never forget.

At Calais I took a place in a coupe – the end compartment of a carriage which, for an extra ten francs, you may have to yourself. There are no arms dividing it into seats, so you can lie down full length and try to get some sleep. I had almost started slumbering away when I was suddenly hurled across the compartment by a terrific jolt. I scrambled to my feet and found the floor of the carriage tilted at 45 degrees; clearly we were off the rails. There was an enormous bruise on my leg, blood on my face and hands and broken glass sliding across the floor.

I hung on and peered out of the window, hearing a few shouts and a hiss of released steam. The carriage behind mine had been forced up into the air and I was certain it was about to fall over and crush me. We were at Marquise, a small town 16 miles from Calais, our first stopping-place. An empty excursion train, it seemed, had run into us. Incredibly my train too was almost empty, for it was a Sunday night, and the English as a rule do not travel on Sundays. Even so, two people were killed in the carriage where the impact occurred. Very shaken, I was taken by railway officials to a hotel in Marquise, where I spent the night.

I set out for Paris again at midday next day, still thoroughly shocked. It was dark when I arrived; I booked in at the Grand and went straight to bed. I felt better the next day and supporting my aching leg with a stick, I hired a carriage and drove to the Maison Rothschild, Rue Lafitte.

It may astonish my readers to know that within moments of picking myself up off the compartment floor of the crashed train it was already occurring to me that the president of the Chemin de Fer du Nord, the railway from Paris to Calais, was Baron Alphonse de Rothschild, head of the Paris Rothschilds, a fact I might turn to my advantage. This thought was very much in my mind when I mounted the steps of the palatial Rothschild building with some difficulty on my stick, entered the English Department, and sat down.

When the manager came over to see me I apologised for not standing, explaining that I had been in the Marquise train crash. This of course had been widely reported in the previous day's newspapers.

"My dear Mr. Warren!" he exclaimed. "How terrible! You have been cut, I see. And your leg!"

"I'll get over it," I said. "It's bruised and painful, but nothing appears to be broken."

After a lot more profuse sympathy he said: "How can we help you in a business way?"

"I would like to see the Baron, if you will."

The manager immediately hurried off. I felt reasonably certain I wouldn't have got away with that one had I not been injured on the Baron's railway, but life is about taking your lucky chances. But instead of being ushered into a plush office I suddenly found myself confronted with a slight, sallow man of about 45, wearing an old-fashioned stovepipe hat and a shabby, snuff-coloured suit. You only had to look at the expression on the faces of the staff milling around to realise that their deity was before me.

"Mr. Warren, please do not get up, because I understand you are hurt," the Baron said, slowly removing his antiquated *chapeau*. "Please accept my most profound apologies for this event. You know, this kind of accident on the railway is very rare in France and we are about to begin an inquiry into it. I intend to instruct my personal doctor to take care of your injuries, and this will be without the slightest charge or expense to yourself."

He went on for a lot longer in that vein, then said: "You are to command me if I can serve you."

I thanked him for his kindness and told him I was still too badly shaken to complete the business for which I had come to Paris. Could he, however, instruct his staff to help me transmit the funds I had brought from

London back again. He called the manager and told him to do anything I requested, then, shaking hands with many more expressions of regret, he withdrew.

I told the manager I wanted a three months' bill on London for £6,000.

"Oh, dear," said this fellow. "I'm afraid the house of Rothschild is not issuing time bills. No matter, the Baron's order suspends that ruling in your case, so I will certainly get you six bills for £1,000 right away."

That of course was just as good for any purpose as one bill for £6,000, but I knew it wouldn't satisfy George.

"I'm sorry," I said. "That won't do. I must have one bill for £6,000."

The manager now looked decidedly vexed. "That is quite unusual, Mr Warren. Perhaps I should explain to you the nature of a bill ..."

"I'm much obliged, but I don't need an explanation. I'm perfectly familiar with the financial world. Perhaps I may ask you to recall the Baron at once."

Just the thought of that clearly sent a thrill of fear through the manager. "Very well, sir, if you insist on the £6,000 in one bill, I will arrange it. But it will involve some delay."

"Never mind the delay," I said. "Here is 150,000 francs on account. and will you please send the bill to the Grand Hotel at 2 p.m. sharp." With no further ado I drove off to the Louvre and spent two hours looking at the excellent pictures there.

At 2 p.m. I was back at the hotel to meet the messenger from Rothschilds with the bill.

"You may like to take a look at the signature on it, sir," said the messenger, smiling. The signature, he pointed out, belonged to a cabinet minister equal in rank to the U.S. Secretary of the Treasury, certifying that the tax due to the government on the bill was paid.

"The revenue stamp needed on a bill of exchange here is one-eighth of one per cent of the face of the bill," the messenger explained. "This makes the tax on your single bill 187 francs. All bills are stamped in a registering machine, which presses the stamp into the paper, but there are no registering machines for a stamp of so high a denomination as 187 francs anywhere in France, so the Baron took the bill to the Treasury himself and got the cabinet minister to sign it."

It was we both agreed, probably the first time in history that such a thing had been done. I wanted very much indeed to keep that bill as a curiosity, but there were better uses for it, and at that time I wasn't a collector of curios.

Even more satisfying was the fact that I had been only 18 hours in Paris and the business for which I had set aside two weeks was already finished. Before leaving London I had planned to get an interview by strategy with the Baron on my arrival in Paris, but it was a pretty hopeless cause, since I had no references and no business introductions in Paris. Amazingly, the providential train accident at Marquise had smoothed the way for me.

So incredible did all this seem to Mac and George that at first they flatly refused to believe it. Only when they saw the bill, holding it to the light, studying it for several minutes, did they accept that I wasn't spoofing them. When they let it go at last, I took it down to the Bank's Burlington branch in St. Swithin's Lane, leaving it for acceptance. When I called next day I found scrawled across it in thin, pale ink the mystic words: "Accepted. Lionel Rothschild."

The bill itself was drawn on cheap blue paper on the same form as the blank bills you could buy at the Paris stationers where in fact I had bought some before leaving for Calais. The acceptance was so simple and easy that Mac copied it on to another bill within ten minutes. That done I set off for the Bank of England for my last personal interview with the manager.

8

WE HIT THE BANK OF ENGLAND

I must now introduce you to the new member we decided at this time to bring into our firm.

He was Edwin Noyes, an old school friend of mine who lived in Hartford, Connecticut, a reserved, discreet and steady sort of chap. He was the man we decided should be our "safe man", acting as my clerk and messenger.

You will have noticed that up to this point I was the only one of our party known to the Bank, so that in the event of our getting caught out it would be necessary only for me to flee. Now we decided on an extra ploy to make matters absolutely safe for me.

I told the manager of the Bank that I had bought a huge plant and shops in Birmingham to manufacture railway material, and that I needed to be there superintending the work a great deal. This meant that I might occasionally send any bills I had for discount by mail from Birmingham. In fact I had already sent two or three lots of genuine bills in that way. We had reasoned that if I could send the forged bills in the same way Mac and George could carry on the business through the post in my name and I could be on the other side of the world while the actual operation was going on. So far from my ever being proved guilty, there would be proof of my innocence, for how could I be guilty of a crime committed in England at the very time I was on a pleasure jaunt in the West Indies or wherever?

The problem for me was that if it all blew up fifty

people in and about the Bank would remember my face. But if I brought a man on to the scene to act as my clerk I need only introduce him to two people: first, to the paying teller of the Bank, and second to the clerk of Jay Cooke and Co., the American banking house where I planned to buy enormous quantities of United States bonds, paying for them in cheques on the Bank of England. These bonds, being bearer bonds, would be as good as so much cash.

I therefore wrote this letter to my old school pal Edwin Noyes.

Grosvenor Hotel,
London, 8 Nov., 1872

My dear Noyes: You will be surprised to hear from me from London, but the fact is I have been here with George and a friend of ours for a year, and have made a lot of money from several speculations we have embarked upon. In fact we have been so successful that we have determined to make you a present of a thousand dollars, which find enclosed.

We may be able to give you a chance to make a few thousands if you care to venture across the ocean. Perhaps we can make use of you. If so, I will send you a cable. If I do, come anyway, as we will pay all your expenses should you determine not to go in with us on the deal. Be cautious and preserve absolute secrecy when you leave home as to your destination. Will explain the reason for this when we meet. The cable may come an hour after you have this.

Hoping you are quite well, I remain, etc., etc.

Two days later we sent him this cable:

"Edwin Noyes, New York. Come by Atlantic on Wednesday, wire on arrival at Liverpool, meet at Langham."

When he arrived we gave him a little dinner party, and over the brandy told him what the score was. He was simply astounded. All next day he behaved like a man in a dream. We all became pretty worried. Was he with us or against us, and if against us, would he thoughtlessly betray us? We hadn't even considered that he might turn us down; now it seemed that he would, and if he did he would be in full knowledge of a vital secret.

What we hadn't realised was that we had become accustomed by degrees to look upon our frauds with equanimity, and Edwin Noyes needed some time himself to become accustomed to them. So it was that after a day or two of silence he began to ask questions about our methods. His mind gradually became more and more familiarised to the thought until finally, fascinated by it all, he said simply: "Right, I need money as badly as you do. I'm with you."

I sent him off to register at an obscure hotel in Manchester Square, with orders to buy some clothes more suitable to his new position than the suit he was wearing from New York.

During the previous few weeks I had several times visited Jay Cooke and Co. in Lombard Street and bought bonds in the name of F. A. Warren, paying with cheques drawn on the Bank of England. Now I went there with Noyes to buy $20,000 in bonds, giving my cheque for them. As the transaction was taking place I introduced Noyes as my clerk, directing them to deliver any bonds I bought to him at any time. Next day Noyes called at the firm, and they gave him the bonds for which 24 hours earlier I had given my cheque. Now there was no need any longer for me to go in person to make purchases. Noyes could appear there any time, give an order for bonds, secure a bill for them, and in half an hour bring a Warren cheque for the amount of the bill, pretending of course that he had got it from me, but in reality getting it from Mac, leaving the cheque for collection and calling next day for the bonds.

The same day I presented Noyes to Jay Cooke and Co. I also took him to the Bank of England at a busy time of day and while drawing £2,000 I casually introduced him to the paying teller as my clerk, asking the teller to pay him any cheques I sent. Then for the next him order two or three small lots of bonds from Jay Cooke and Co., so that they got to know him coming on my business.

I now set off for the Bank of England for my last visit, with the Rothschild bill in my pocket. Some remarkably exaggerated stories were subsequently published in the newspapers about this famous interview, so let me relate exactly what happened. When I arrived at the Bank I was ushered into the manager's office. I put the bill on his desk.

"You will notice that it is signed by a French cabinet minister," I observed. "He certifies that the internal revenue tax has been paid on it."

The manager picked it up and studied it. "This is remarkable," he said. "I don't believe I have ever seen anything like it before."

When I told him that the Baron himself had authorised it he was clearly very impressed. The unusualness of the bill led him to digress into some of the more uncommon things that had happened while he was at the Bank, and bold as brass, I decided to ask him a direct question.

"Do you ever come across any kinds of forgery?"

"Ah, no, Mr. Warren. Forgery against the Bank is impossible."

"Why so? Other banks get hit sometimes, why not the Bank of England?"

I can't remember his exact reply, except that it was extremely long-winded, and ended: "Our wise forefathers have bequeathed to us a system which is perfect."

"Your forefathers?" I echoed, smiling in mock disbelief. "Do you seriously mean that you haven't changed the system since the time of your forefathers?"

"Not in the slightest particular for a hundred years," he replied.

Chuckling to myself, I changed the subject.

"I shall be fully occupied for many months ahead looking after my different business interests," I said. "But if I have time I will certainly call by and see you. Now I wonder if I may have the bill discounted and take the cash with me, instead of having it placed to my credit."

"Certainly, Mr. Warren." He summoned a clerk, gave the order, and the cash was handed to me. We shook hands, and I went fleet-footed to our meeting-place, where I showed Mac and George the notes I'd been given for the discounted bill.

"No more tests, I hope?" I said, eyeing George. They both laughed. We were at last ready to go. The first move was for me to get out of England. We had our farewell dinner, drank a little too much, talked about the happy future – about our four-in-hands, our summer cottages at Saratoga and Newport, our town house, fine suppers and boxes at the opera. Over the brandies we squared up our cash account, all of us agog at the way our money had melted away. For the benefit of Noyes we did some reminiscing about our European and South American trips.

"Did you ever lose confidence?" Noyes asked.

"Only once," I told him. "That was in Rio, when the letter "c" in lieu of the letter "s" sent our sure thing down the tubes."

"We were really up against fate that day," Mac said, shaking his head over that piece of bad judgement.

What I didn't say that evening was from that moment I sometimes wondered if that letter "c" were an omen. Certainly I had a constant feeling from that time on that the short-cuts we were taking to a fortune were highly risky. But confidence always comes in good company, and when we were all together again, under the stimulus of our friendship I forgot all my foreboding and became quite convinced that the unseen fatal something could never happen. We had covered our tracks so well, taken care of every possible emergency, that any kind of mishap was now inconceivable.

The day after our dinner, it was a Monday, I loaded my packed bags into a cab, shook hands warmly with my accomplices, and set out for Victoria Station, Dover and Calais. I had every reason to feel pleased with myself, for as soon as I arrived in Paris I planned to marry. My fiancée was an English girl, Jane, the daughter of a minor diplomat stationed in Paris, and we had met on my previous visits to France. If I've told you nothing of this in the past and if I don't want to dwell for long on our romance and our wedding now, you will readily understand when you have heard all my story. Jane's background was impeccable; just about the last man she could ever have envisaged marrying was an international confidence trickster, and when as my wife the painful truth was revealed to her I know how much it hurt.

The first lot of forged bills were posted from Birmingham on Wednesday that week, giving me forty-eight hours to get out of the country. Our first thought had been to recoup our enormous expenses, so it had been agreed that the first batch of bills shouldn't exceed the amount we had spent since leaving Rio. This account of what happened after my departure I have put together partly from what my accomplices afterwards told me, and partly from newspaper reports.

On Wednesday of that week Noyes went to the Bank and drew out all the money to my credit, except for £300. The same day he went to Birmingham and mailed lot number one of our home-made bills, to a value of £8,000.

The next 18 hours was an anxious time for my friends. The bills would be delivered by the early post on Thursday, and if all went right the proceeds would be placed to my credit by midday, and the bills themselves would be stowed away in the vaults until they were due some months ahead. As a precaution Mac and George had everything packed for instant flight, but the only way they would know that the fraud had worked would be to make a test. Accordingly, they filled out two Warren cheques, one for £2,300 payable to Warren, and the other for £4.10s., payable to bearer.

Noyes took the cheques, with the other two following some distance behind him, and placed himself on the steps of a hotel in a side street not far from the Bank, watching the passers-by. Finally he stopped a uniformed messenger. He asked the fellow to take the £4. 10s. cheque to the Bank, bring the money back to him, and told him he would be paid for his trouble.

As soon as the messenger had gone Noyes sprinted around the corner to a place agreed upon, while Mac followed the messenger to the Bank and saw he was paid without question. He made a prearranged signal to George, who went to tell Noyes, who returned to his position on the hotel steps in time for the messenger's return with the money.

Mac, George and Noyes now started for the Bank. Noyes went in, and nodding good-day to the cashier, presented the cheque for £2,300.

"Could I have £2,000 in gold and the remainder in notes, please?" he asked. This was handed to him without demur.

That evening my three friends sat down to dinner in a convivial mood. They had conclusively proved that the Bank of England's methods were fallible.

Next day Noyes went to Jay Cooke and Co, and ordered $75,000 in United States bonds, giving a cheque for them on the Bank. The same afternoon he went to Birmingham and posted another letter containing £15,000 in bills, and later drew £2,000 in gold from the Bank. On Monday – this was a week after my departure – he went after the bonds, and the $75,000 was handed over to him without question. The whole operation then became a repetition of these tactics, with an ever-increasing volume in the amounts of the bills. On some days the post brought to the Bank letters with bills for $100,000, sometimes for more, sometimes for less.

Thus November and December passed, and the Bank continued day by day and week by week laying away in its vaults the worthless collateral of Mr. F. A. Warren in exchange for its gold.

As Christmas drew nearer Mac was longing for home. He hadn't been getting on too well with his father when he left America; there had been a reconciliation by mail, and now each post brought letters from his family looking forward to the day when he would return. But the argument to stay in London, and it prevailed, was that the money was coming in so easily and in such large amounts that it would be idiotic to run away from it. There was another thought – that by obtaining an enormous sum and putting it in a place of absolute security the Bank, if they found out, would be glad to compromise the matter in consideration of receiving a million or two back again.

So they spent a pretty merry and an exceedingly expensive Christmas in London, but in February they determined to pack up and leave. And why not? The gold and bonds had meant fortunes for us all. I was then on a steamship in the tropics, leading an idle life with my bride. Mac and George had never appeared in any of our business, and as for Noyes, no one in America knew he was in Europe, and in Europe only three or four people had seen him and knew him as representing Warren. When they left England with the loot the Bank would slumber on for a few weeks until the first bills became due and chaos descended.

They held a meeting, and agreed that the last batch of bills posted from Birmingham would in fact be the last they sent. That meant just one more day and the strain on their nerves would be over. That day Noyes bought bonds and drew cash for more than $150,000. At 3 o'clock they sat down to lunch, their last in London, then went to Mac's apartments in St. James' Place to burn or destroy all the material he had there for making forged bills. Mac, as the artist who had executed the actual writing, began throwing the unused bills on to the fire. Occasionally he set aside some bill more elaborate than the common run on the floor beside his chair. When he had finished he was about to crumple up and throw the elaborate few on the floor into the fire, too, when he suddenly decided to smooth some of them out for a last look .

"These are perfect works of art," he mused. "It's such a pity to destroy them."

"We only have to post them," Noyes said. "They'll bring us in thousands of pounds."

"Let's send them in," George said. "We've nothing to lose now."

A letter was hurriedly written, the bills, with memorandum, enclosed, and all three of them went off to Birmingham, where they posted the letter.

The following morning, a Tuesday, the bills arrived at the Bank. Following the routine, they went to the discount department, were discounted and placed to my credit. As I then had a balance of £20,000, when the proceeds of the bills were added to it my credit was £46,000.

But a strange thing had happened. In the discount department a clerk noticed that the date was missing from one of the bills. The omission was made on an acceptance of Blydenstein and Co., a large banking firm in London. The clerk, thinking it was no more than a clerical error on the part of the bookkeeper of Blydenstein and Co., made no report about it. He discounted the bill with the other eighteen, put seventeen of the bills in the vaults with the batches which had preceded them, and put the eighteenth, the one with the missing date, aside. At 10.30 the next morning, Wednesday, he gave the bill to the bank messenger, telling him when he went his regular rounds to take the bill to Blydenstein's and ask them to correct the omission.

A left-off date! Even now, when I think of it a quarter of a century later, I have to put down my pen in utter disbelief. For in those simple, routine office procedures carried out that morning by the discount clerk and the Bank messenger, the wheels which were to grind our scheme into ruins were set in motion.

At 2 p.m. on Tuesday, the day before this happened, Noyes went to Jay Cooke and Co. and ordered $100,000 in United States bonds, and gave them a cheque on the Bank of England for the amount. He was to call for the bonds next day of course, after the cheque had gone through the Clearing House and had been paid.

At 9.30 a.m. on Wednesday, Noyes ran his usual test by sending in a messenger with a small cheque. The money was paid as usual – which was a complete demonstration that everything was all right. It was all right at 9.30, but an hour later the Bank messenger started off for Blydenstein's with our fatal bill.

The bills had now been in the Bank's possession for twenty-four hours, had been discounted, and the proceeds placed to my credit. So Noyes went to Jay Cooke and Co. and as the cheque had been paid at the Bank they handed over to him, as on so many other occasions, the $100,000 in bonds.

Mac and George were outside. George took the bonds and gave Noyes a cheque for £10,000. A minute after leaving Jay Cooke, Noyes was at the Bank counter. The cashier counted out the cash for him against his cheque and Noyes walked out on to the grey street. He was jubilant. He would never have to go to the Bank again.

He walked quickly to meet Mac and George at the famous Garraway's coffee house in Exchange Alley and sitting down together at 10.35 they reminded themselves that their income that morning was $140,000, plus all the other cash they had made from the Bank in the previous months.

"I'm never going back to the Bank again!" said Noyes, laughing. "Let's shake hands on that."

They all clasped hands solemnly. At that moment the Bank messenger was rushing past Garraway's on his way to tell the Bank that Mr. Warren's £2,000 bill, discounted yesterday, was a forgery.

One can imagine what happened when he got to Blydenstein's and asked a clerk to put the date on the bill. One glance would have told the clerk that the bill, on his company's paper, wasn't one of theirs. He would have said something like this to the messenger: "You had better tell your masters not to discount this. It isn't ours, so it must be a forgery."

One can imagine, too, the look of unbelief when the messenger, hot-footing it back to the Bank and presenting the bill to the manager, told him that Blydenstein's said it was a forgery.

A forgery? But it's Mr. Warren's bill ...

Mr. Warren?

I afterwards learned that from that moment chaos reigned in the Bank of England. The police were called, and swarms of them poured out of Bow Street and the Scotland Yard offices. All was confusion and excitement. All that a couple of officials could blabber out to the police was something about a tall young man, an American who said his name was Warren. Within minutes the story was in Fleet Street, where it was quickly magnified into gigantic frauds affecting every bank in London. There was babbling excitement on the Stock Exchange floor when a messenger brought in the news. And while the financial centre of the mighty British Empire was twisting and shuddering in turmoil, my three friends, oblivious to the tumult only a few yards away, were metaphorically slapping themselves on their backs over their coffee.

Had they known about it, they would have had time to fade quietly out of England. They didn't know, and that was their undoing. Casually pouring himself another coffee, Mac remarked: "It's almost too bad that we're pulling out leaving a balance of $75,000 at the Bank to Warren's credit."

Noyes nearly dropped his coffee cup.

"Seventy-five grand?" he exclaimed. "That's ridiculous! We're not going to leave that kind of money to John Bull. We'll take some of it with us. Make out a cheque for £5,000. I'll run over and pick up the cash, we'll use it for pocket money."

Ah, Noyes, if you hadn't been quite so cocksure at that moment! But ours is not a business where recriminations serve any purpose whatsoever. Mac wrote the cheque, Noyes ran to the Bank with it, was instantly recognised by the clerk, and was besieged as if he had poked a red-hot stick into a nest of hornets. There were 25 detectives on the premises, and the Bank parlour was packed with stockholders and directors.

With almost the fervour of an American lynch mob, they descended on my luckless associate. They dragged him into a private office and pinning his arms, plied him with questions.

Noyes wouldn't be shaken; his nerve never once failed him. He babbled out something about a gentleman having hired him as a clerk, and that was all he knew. He had left the gentleman at the Stock Exchange, if they would let him he would try and find the man and bring him around to the Bank. There was no way they were going to take him up on that. Instead they escorted him to Newgate Prison.

9

THE BIRDS SCATTER IN ALL DIRECTIONS

While all that was happening inside the Bank, Mac and George, still waiting outside, were growing more and more anxious by the second, for the swarming crowd, the excited people rushing in and out, was telling its own dreadful story. Taking advantage of the confusion, Mac slipped into the Bank and saw through a half - opened door Noyes being interrogated by a group of angry officials.

Mac made sure that Noyes saw him, as if to reassure him that he would do all he could, then he rushed back to George. Could they rescue Noyes from the mob while he was being taken to prison? This was desperate stuff. They joined in with the crowd, but although Noyes could see them they just couldn't get close enough to him, which in the event was just as well. With sinking hearts they watched the great gate of the Newgate jail close on him.

That afternoon Noyes had a visitor to his cell. It was Lionel Rothschild, president of the Bank's board of directors, ready to offer the prisoner his freedom and £1,000 if he would tell all he knew. Noyes shook his head. A gentleman, an entire stranger, had hired him as a clerk and messenger, and he knew nothing about Mr. Warren or his business.

While Mac and George were tailing the Newgate mob, the bag containing the $150,000 drawn that morning was behind the counter at Garraway's. As Mac went in to retrieve it, one of the waitresses asked him if he had heard about the great Bank robbery. Nodding his head with a forced grin, he picked up the bag and drove to St. James' Place, where George joined him.

Now there was time for an hour's cool reflection. They came eventually to two conclusions, one that Noyes would never betray us, and two, that he could never be convicted of forgery. He might have to suffer a few weeks in Newgate, which was unfortunate, but it would come out all right. So they would hang about in London and await developments.

Next morning's world press overflowed with the story of the fraud and its perpetrator, known only as F. A. Warren, an American. Some of the newspaper comment made amusing reading. They were full of Philistine talk and amazement. They generally conceded that Noyes was an innocent dupe, and all doubted if his principal, the mysterious Mr. F. A. Warren, would ever come back to say so.

As day followed day Mac and George hung around London reading the accounts of the affair and of the examination of Noyes before the Lord Mayor. They managed to communicate with him through his solicitor, and his brief reply was that they should leave England at once. Eschewing this advice, they continued each day to send off to American addresses the cash they had made. They were so convinced that by no possible chance could their names become involved in the affair that in every instance but two they sent the money or bonds to America in their own names.

In the meantime the Bank had cabled its New York legal agent, Clarence A. Seward, asking him to alert the American detective force. Seward knew the sort of men who ruled at Police Headquarters, so he sent for Robert Pinkerton, whose private detective agency was world-renowned.*

---

* The Pinkerton detective agency was founded in Chicago in 1852 by Allan Pinkerton and became world-famous under his two sons, Robert and William, solving many sensational criminal cases.

The first thing Pinkertons did was to lead our friends Jimmy Irving and Co to believe the case would be entirely a matter for the New York Police Headquarters, and to strengthen this belief they had the Bank of England agent in New York go to Police Headquarters every day and pretend to consult with Irving.

Reading the cable dispatches in the press about what we had done, the bliss of Irving and his men was ecstatic, for each of them saw themselves with a new diamond pin and rig, the proceeds of their springing to our defence. But the lawyers and the Pinkertons between them played Irving and Police Headquarters for fools and knaves. Day after day one of the lawyers, having first been tutored by Pinkerton, went to Mulberry Street and gave deceptive information to Irving, who, with his two chums, was completely hoodwinked.

Back in London Noyes was examined by magistrates almost every day, but remained silent. Searching him, the London police found his suits were made by a London tailor with several shops. Two Pinkerton men arriving in London from New York to pick up the case were given this information, and discovered not only which shop Noyes had patronised, but that he had given the name Bedford. Why a false name, they asked? This was a bad mark against Noyes.

One of the salesmen remembered seeing Mr. Bedford walking in Mayfair one day with a tall, handsome gentleman of whom he was able to give a good description. This, unfortunately for us, was Mac. The detectives started to make a house-to-house search in Mayfair. They soon enough came to the house of a famous London doctor named Payson Hewitt, of whom Mac had been a patient. All that Dr. Hewitt knew about him was the address he gave, Westminster Palace Hotel. Inquiries revealed Mac had never stayed there, but even so, the Pinkerton men were elated, because with a fictitious name and a fictitious address they knew they were on to something.

Then Dr. Hewitt suddenly remembered something else: Mac had told him he was a medical graduate from an American university. A check on U. S. medical school records was all that was now needed to build up a complete profile of George Macdonnell and his friends.

Knowing none of this, Mac and George decided to return to America. Mac was to go by way of Paris, and the last thing he did before leaving his lodgings in St. James' Place, was to roll up in three rolls $254,000 in United States bonds and send the trunk containing them by express to Major George Mathews, New York. He wrapped them up in a nightshirt belonging to me which in some way had got into his baggage. Then he bought a ticket to Paris and sent his baggage over, waiting in London a day or two longer before going himself. In Paris he registered at the Hotel Richmond, in the Rue du Helder under his right name.

George decided to go by way of Ireland, and as with his earlier adventures in France, he afterwards recounted his amazing adventures there, which I will presently let him tell in his own language.

In London the Pinkertons were nothing if not lucky. Knocking on every door in St. James' Place they came to Mac's lodgings. His landlady was furious when she heard their purpose; she would have nothing said against the nice American gentleman. When the Bank's solicitors and some other important people came to see her, though, she opened up a bit, and what she told them must have been of considerable value. She had seen a great deal of me, though she had never heard my name, but the detectives knew from my description that she was talking about F. A. Warren.

Mac's rooms had been unoccupied since he left, so they were able to make a worthwhile search. In the still unemptied wastepaper basket they found some odd pieces of blotting paper which, when held to the light revealed writing the same as on the written sheet. And one piece had this to say:

Ten thousand Pounds Sterling.

F. A. Warren.

The handwriting compared exactly with a cancelled cheque of mine at the Bank, and as a piece of evidence it told against Mac, for it bound him hard and fast to me, who was already bound to Noyes.

"Where has Mr. Macdonnell gone to?" they asked the landlady.

"Why, sir, I believe he said he would go to Paris on business," she replied.

In Paris, Pinkerton and his assistant went to the American bankers where most Americans register on arrival, and found Mac's name there as large as life, registered at Andrews and Co's as stopping at the Hotel Richmond. If anyone should wonder why Mac was using his name so openly they should remember he had absolutely no reason to suspect that he could be associated with Noyes. And so unsuspecting, he bought a ticket from the Paris agency of a steamship company for the *Thuringia,* a steamer due to sail from Brest.

To the Hotel Richmond went Pinkerton, and from there to the ticket agency. A wire to Brest to arrest Mac as he boarded the ship arrived just too late – the *Thuringia* had sailed half an hour earlier. Pinkerton was by now quite relaxed; he had only to cable his associates in New York to have Mac arrested as the ship docked. That gave him plenty of time to turn his attention to me.

And there he had a mountain to climb, for very few people knew where I was, and certainly neither Mac, George nor Noyes knew.

On the other hand, it seemed that almost everyone in New York quickly knew where Mac was. Still unsuspecting, he had cabled Irving that he was arriving by the *Thuringia,* and would the police chief kindly meet him at the port. Pinkerton, feeling that no secrecy was required about his quarry being on the steamer, gave the story to the press, and Irving discovered, to his fury, that all the world shared with him the secret of Mac's whereabouts.

This meant that to save his reputation he would have to be on hand not as a friend or confederate but in his official capacity to make a genuine arrest, that is, unless he could arrange to have Mac taken off the steamer in a small boat as soon as she came into the lower bay and before the official police boat arrived. This task he decided to give to a chum, Johnny Dobbs, who had earned Irving's considerable friendship through his abilities as a high-class burglar.

Dobbs turned out to be a much better burglar than kidnapper of wanted men. He hired his boat and patrolled the harbour, but unfortunately went ashore on Staten Island for a tea break just as the *Thuringia* slipped into port.

When Irving heard the ship had arrived he deliberately kept the official police boat, containing five U.S. Marshals, bank officials and private detectives, waiting an hour, then, supposing Mac was safely ashore, boarded the ship ahead of them with his two cronies, White and Stanley. Irving saw Mac on deck first and rapidly explained the state of affairs. Mac's reaction was characteristic.

"Come down to my stateroom," he said. "I've got something for you."

In the stateroom he gave them several packets. "These are $150,000 in bonds, and $10,000 in greenbacks, which I bought off the brokers in London," he said. "And here are some English banknotes, and three valuable diamonds." Taking out several bags of sovereigns, he went on: "Help yourselves. Take as much as you can carry. Load yourselves up – the important thing is to keep as much as possible from the enemy."

Irving and Co. dived into the gold, with the furious police-boat officials only yards away still awaiting his permission to board. Their big problem was that any bulging pockets would quickly be noticed, so they had to leave much more than they could take. I can tell you

Standing opposite the Bank of England (above) I said to my companions, "That's the one we should bust" (Chapter 1)

Followed by an angry mob, Noyes was escorted to Newgate Prison (Chapter 8)

A Bidwell- faked version of the bill of exchange for £6,000 signed
by Alphonse de Rothschild in Paris (Chapter 7)

**Henry Hawkins QC
Leading Counsel
for the Crown**

**Sir J. Mellor
Justice of the
Queen's Bench**

**Sir A.J.E. Cockburn
Lord Chief Justice
of England**

The Lord Chancellor.

Sir C. Russell QC

Queen's Counsel.

Witnesses.

*Clerk of
the Old Bailey.*

"I object My Lord"

Sketches made at the Old Bailey trial

The swarming crowd outside the Bank was telling its own dreadful story to Mac and George (Chapter 9)

**An adjournment during the Old Bailey trial of the
conspirators**

The set of drawings on this and the following pages depicting scenes from Austin Bidwell's extraordinary life were found among his papers after his death. Since they were unsigned, and both George Macdonnell and George Bidwell were accomplished artists, one of them may have been responsible for them. The sketch of the trial participants at the Old Bailey must have been made by someone in court, so this too, could have been drawn by either of the two artists

I pointed to the Bank of England and said to my companions, "That's the one we should bust" (Chapter 1)

Noyes ran into the Bank and was besieged by a crowd exhibiting all the fervour of an American lynch mob (Chapter 8)

"Help yourselves," Mac told the detectives, pointing to the money. "Take as much as you can " (Chapter 9)

Three or four shots rang out and our train came to a shuddering stop (Chapter 11)

The captain seized a bayonet hanging on the wall and came at me like a mad bull (Chapter 13)

The door to Newgate Prison.
"The sight of the grim fortress,
a prison for 500 years, sent a
cold shiver through me"
(Chapter 14)

"Come out, Bidwell!"
Ross shouted, as the
cell door swung open
(Chapter 17)

from long association with Jimmy Irving that that would really have hurt.

Down at the bottom of the companion-way the police and marshals had become so exasperated that they decided not to wait for Irving's permission to board any longer, and virtually stormed the ship. When they arrived at Mac's stateroom they found Irving, White and Stanley with their prisoner under arrest.

"You'd better search the stateroom," Irving said smoothly. "We haven't had time to go through it."

The marshals searched every inch of space and were soon back on deck in triumph, carrying around £5,000 in sovereigns. Poor old Irving! How he must have hated that moment.

As for the prisoner, no one expected to find anything on him. As it was he had $20, which everyone thought Irving must have overlooked.

Of course, none of the rest of us knew what was happening to Mac at that time; indeed, none of us even knew where he was. George was in Ireland and not reading newspapers, Noyes was in Newgate jail, and I was some place where no one was going to find me. Had we known we would have had sadly to acknowledge that Mac looked as if he was done for. He was turned over to United States officials and put in Ludlow Street jail pending an examination before the United States Commissioner with a view to his extradition.

While the legal debates about his future wrangled on and on, as lawyers like them to, the Pinkertons were unearthing the $254,000 wrapped in my nightshirt in Mac's trunk at the European Express Office, 44 Broadway. Circulars were sent out to the banks and trust companies warning them to hold all funds deposited by any of our party. The fatal piece of blotting paper was produced in a New York court, which finally decreed that Mac should be given up to the British Government to stand trial for complicity in the great Bank of England forgery.

All this took three months, but it still wasn't quite over. Mac, transferred to Fort Columbus, hung on in, arguing on writs of habeas corpus and certiorari to the Supreme Court. He lost all along the way, and then the U.S. Government seemed to become exceedingly tired of him, for with scarcely time to say good-bye to his counsel he was suddenly driven down Broadway to the Battery under armed police guard and transferred to Governor's Island by tug. From there he was taken the following day to the other end of the island, where the tugboat *Schultze* was waiting for him.

News had spread quickly that a distinguished prisoner was about to leave his native shores, and a large crowd of soldiers and civilians lined the wharf. They saw a man who didn't seem a bit fussed, smoking, laughing, and clearly in a state of unaccountable good humour. They saw him board the *Schultze,* which rattled off down the Bay to the steamer *Minnesota,* lying at anchor near Pier 46, North River. There two English detective sergeants named Webb and Hancock received him in custody from the U. S. Marshals. For the present I will leave him on the Atlantic Ocean, sailing eastwards to meet his terrible fate.

10

GEORGE'S ORDEAL IN IRELAND

When Mac left on his ill-fated trip to Paris, George stayed on in London for a few days, long enough to hear the hue and cry gathering momentum. He had, as I have already said, intended to return to America via Ireland, but by the time he decided to buy a ticket he was aware that all the railway stations in London were being watched, and that any single man buying a ticket for America would probably have to give an account of himself.

Adopting extraordinary precautions in the way that only George knew how, he sent a porter to buy a ticket for Dublin via Holyhead, and another ticket on the steamer Atlantic bound from Cork to New York. He waited until the last moment before jumping on the 9 p.m. train, slipping past the loading of the mails, for he reasoned that a couple of soundless fellows loitering around in the waiting-room watching passengers were detectives.

George arrived in Dublin at 7 a.m. after a good night's sleep on the steamer. It might not have been quite so comfortable, perhaps, had he known that the telegraph was flashing in all directions offering £5,000 reward for his capture.

This is the story he afterwards told me:

"On the day in February when I arrived in Dublin a whole column about us was published in the Irish newspapers. I didn't find this out until later because I hadn't bought one. They were not particularly looking for me, they were just watching the ports and rail stations for lone Americans, who were just as likely to leave the British Isles from Ireland as they were from England. So blissfully unsuspecting, I took the train for Queenstown, Cork, a place I'd never been to before, and set out on foot for the port. In my pocket was my ticket for the S.S. *Atlantic*.

"A few yards from the station one of two detectives who were clearly watching the passengers leaving trains, came up to me and said:

"'Have you ever been here before?'

"I gave him a haughty look. 'Of course I have,' I rapped, continuing to walk and not giving him a second glance. He stepped along beside me for a few yards, as if irresolute, then fell back and rejoined his companion.

"I turned away from the harbour, went along the main street and stopped at a chemist's. I wanted to see if I was being followed, and thinking the coast was clear I set off down another street. Quite fortuitously I came to an enclosure with a gate, over which was a sign saying that this was the wharf for the New York steamers.

"There were tugs waiting on the wharf to take passengers out to the Atlantic, but before deciding to board one I took a covert look round. Sure enough, there were the two detectives, eyeing me from one corner of the wharf. I leaned casually on the rail, gazing at the scene, then turned and left the wharf without a glance at the detectives.*

"I walked up a hill, hailed a cab, and asked to be taken to the next station after Queenstown. I bought a ticket there, but as I put it in my pocket I saw my two detectives. The cab was still waiting outside, so I

---

*George was lucky to be able to relate the rest of his tale. When the S.S.Atlantic left Cork for New York later that day she was starting out on her last voyage. Off Nova Scotia she was twenty miles off course and struck the coast at Meager's Head, Prospect Harbour. She broke in two, rolled into deep water, and sank in a few minutes. Of 1,002 people on board 560 were drowned, including most of the saloon passengers and all the women and children.

jumped in and told the driver to take me back to Cork, this time to the station which served Dublin. I hadn't been there many moments, sitting in the waiting-room, when in came the two detectives.

"As soon as a train came in I went on to the platform, and pretended to be looking for a passenger alighting. Acting as if my intended passenger was not on the train, I left the station and walked briskly into the busiest part of the city. As soon as my followers were too far behind to catch me I slipped into a temperance hotel and registered for the night.

"And what a night! I guessed something was wrong, but I had no idea what it was about. I was sure they did not suspect me personally, that they were only tailing anyone who was a stranger, alone, answering a rough description, perhaps, and looking suspicious. I must be filling all these requirements, because they had stuck to me doggedly. Now I had somehow to lose them.

"Early next morning I slipped out and bought a holdall, a Scottish cap and a cheap scarf. I hadn't been back in the hotel for many moments when from the window of the commercial room on the second floor I saw the two detectives walking down the street.

"I quickly put on the things I'd bought, went downstairs and as soon as they had passed the hotel got into a cab. I told the driver to take me to a canal bridge. I walked across the bridge, stopped at a small shop, and tipped a boy to fetch me a jaunting car. Soon I was rolling northwards.

"On the road we passed a group of very poor-looking folk, and I couldn't resist throwing a few coins to them. My driver at once decided I must be a priest; only priests, apparently, give away money in Ireland. He wouldn't be dissuaded from that view, only deciding instead that I must be a priest travelling incognito. When we stopped at a tavern about 12 miles from Cork, and two from Fermoy, he told the mistress of the place that I was a priest who didn't want the fact to be known.

It was a good ploy, because for my short stay I was treated like royalty. But I didn't want the cabbie to go back to Cork until it was dark, so I kept him eating and drinking with me.

"'Fedder,' he kept saying. 'You're a dacent man, so you are,' while I kept one eye anxiously on the setting sun. When it was safe, I sent him on his way, uproariously rejoicing. 'Good-bye, Fedder,' he shouted. 'And God be with you, now.' The mistress of the tavern, overhearing all this nonsense, beamed to think she had such a generous priest among her company.

"I had no intention of staying the night, however. As soon as the cabbie was gone I set out on foot for Fermoy station, taking the hostler to carry my bag. Half a mile from the village I let him return. In the village I bought a new cap, a Glengarry.

"At the station I noticed a man lounging near the ticket office who was clearly watching anyone who bought a ticket. That quickly put Dublin out of my mind, and I bought a ticket for Lismore. I must have fallen asleep on the train, for at Lismore I was the only one on it and the staff were putting out the lights.

"I booked in at the first hotel I could find, the Lismore House, had supper and went into the lounge. There was just one other person there, a chap I took from our brief conversation to be a lawyer. When he bade me goodnight he left his newspaper on the table in front of me, and the first thing I saw was a front-page story in large type offering £5,000 reward for my arrest.

"I was dumbfounded, paralysed, bewildered. I had no doubt that the lawyer had guessed who I was. I went to my room, but long before it was light the next day, Sunday, I was up and downstairs. I carefully turned the key of the front door and crept out on to the piazza, which ran along the front of the hotel. There my worst fears were confirmed – there was a man on the opposite side of the street watching the hotel.

"I decided to play the next round very coolly. When it

was light I went out on to the street and sauntered up towards the shopping centre, like a man taking an airing before breakfast. At every turn I could see I was being followed. Strolling back to the hotel, I decided that Lismore, like Cork, had become too hot for me.

"I stopped at the livery stable and found the hostler just getting up.

"'I need a horse for the day,' I said.

"'They're all engaged, yer honour. Least, they all are save for one, the fastest of them all, and 'e's got such a long journey come Tuesday we're a-letting um rest till then.'

"'But my good fellow, I must have a horse, and at once, with you to drive. There will be half a sovereign for a good Irishman, such as I see before me.'

"The hostler scratched his head. My blarney was beginning to do the trick. 'Well, sir, I'll waken my master the hotel-keeper, and yer honour can talk with um.'

"A night-capped head responded to his rap on the window, and after a few words and a promise of cash the hotelier agreed to let me have the resting horse. Soon we were rattling out of Lismore at the full speed of a blooded Irish horse. Thirty miles away was the village of Clonmel, which was connected to Dublin by a branch line.

"When we were five miles short of the place the rain began to come down in torrents. We stopped at a country grocery store and had some lunch of bread and cheese, and which included a dram of whiskey thrown in gratis. I gave my driver a sovereign, telling him to pay off his master for the hire and keep the change for himself.

"'Yer 'onour's a jintleman and no mistake.'

"When he had gone I asked the storekeeper to get a boy to take me to Clonmel. It was only five miles, but I found out that day why they call Ireland the Green Isle. It was as if buckets of water were being poured over us; my Glengarry and every thread on me was waterlogged. In such a state we arrived at Clonmel, where the boy drove through a high gate into the back yard of a she-been kept by his uncle.

"I was led into a room at the back of the shop, and as I stood drying my clothes by the fire I saw through the half-open door how the thirsty souls of old Erin evade the Sunday liquor law. It was a pantomime to watch, and it took my mind off my own troubles for a short time. The proprietor stood in the shop in a position where he could covertly keep an eye on the policeman patrolling the street, and as soon as that officer was out of sight a signal was given, the back yard gate thrown open, and a dozen men rushed in, the gate closing behind them. Coming past me through the back room into the shop, they all snatched up a 'potheen' and drained it dry.

"It was 2 p.m., and the rain had stopped. I walked along the main street until I saw a sign 'Cabs to let'. I knocked and was shown into an inner room, where the proprietress sat crooning over a turf fire.

"'Will you take a seat?' she asked. And when I had settled myself, 'And what is it you'll be wanting, sir?'

"'I need to go to Caher.' This was about eight miles away. 'I need to hire a cab to take me.'

"'How long will you wish to be gone?'

"'Oh, I don't know. Certainly I shall be back later tonight. I shall be visiting friends, officers stationed in the fort at Caher.'

"'Are you not a American, sir, by your voice?'

"'Oh, no, ma'am, I'm English, though I've often been mistaken for an American. That's because I'm from Norfolk in England, and it was from there that the original Yankees emigrated, taking our accent with them, which is why I have a similar accent to Americans.'

"'I see, I see. Well, you must forgive me for asking, it's of no importance where you're from, because I can see you're all right.' She drew her chair closer to mine. 'The fact is that the captain of police sent an order that I should tell him at once if any stranger wished to hire a vehicle, especially if I thought him an American. But you know, sir, I don't care for those dogs of police, they are all a parcel of spies and informers in the pay of the English Government. So you may depend upon it that even if you were the one they were looking for they shall wait a long time for me to tell them, and you shall have my best horse and driver.'

"'Well, ma'am, you are too kind, indeed you are. I shall remember your kindness to me, and that of all your countrymen.'

"Arriving in Caher, I paid the driver and sent him back. As I walked up the main street I looked back over my shoulder. A cab being driven furiously was coming through the town gate I had just entered. It dashed up the street and pulled up a few yards from me. As two constables jumped out I turned quickly into a narrow lane through which I could see the entrance gateway to Caher fort.

"A sentry was pacing up and down; opposite the entrance were two ruined cottages. As the sentry turned away from me I slipped into one of the cottages, pinning myself against a wall.

"I could hear all that was happening outside. I heard the constables stop the sentry.

"'Have you seen a man around here?'

"'No one, sir.'

"'We believe a man may have slipped through the gate while your back was turned.'

"'That's not possible, sir. I would've seen him, for sure I would.'

"'We'd better talk to your captain. Lead us to him.'

"I heard the sentry go off with them, and presently all three returned, the constables obviously going off towards the main street. But I dared not move. I stayed breathlessly in that ruin for two more hours, then crept out and merged unseen by the sentry into the night.

"I was now desperate. I had to find some cover, and quickly. Almost instinctively, I knocked at the first front door I saw. It was opened to reveal a family eating their supper. In the true spirit of Irish hospitality I was invited in at once.

"'Sir,' I said, addressing the father of the house, who told me his name was Maloy. 'I need help. I'm a Fenian* leader, and the police are searching for me. I have papers which I must get to other Fenians urgently. I must get out of Caher and back to Clonmel without being seen.'

"At that moment a carriage came rumbling by outside. 'You're in luck,' said Maloy. 'There goes the mail car to the post-office. Come with me.'

"He stepped out into the street and hailed down the mail, a jaunting car. He told the driver, who was a friend, my problem, and with no further ado I was whisked off into the night aboard the mail car. The driver dropped me off at a tavern near Clonmel railway station, where, too late to move on, I found the only food they had was eggs. After a sleepless night and a day on the move with hardly anything to eat, I had to settle for those eggs; I won't tell you how many, because I'm sure you wouldn't believe me. Then, filled with eggs, I set off for the railway station, caught the 11 p.m. train to Dublin, and arrived there at one o'clock in the morning.

"I could see several loiterers whom I took to be detectives outside the station, so I slipped out via a back way. Even so, as soon as I got into a cab I could see it was being followed. By ordering my cabbie around innumerable turnings and corners we managed to shake off our tail. That done, I booked into the Cathedral Hotel for a couple of hours.

"If you think I was imagining my followers, let me tell you what happened when during the afternoon, after I'd paid my hotel bill and left, I stopped to buy some old clothes in the market quarter. The saleslady on the stall

---

*The real name of the Fenian Society was the Irish Republican Brotherhood, and its object was to overthrow British rule in Ireland.

looked at me curiously, obviously intrigued at seeing a well-dressed man making such purchases. I thought I should put her mind at ease.

"'A Fenian friend has got himself into a scrape, and the police are after him,' I explained. "So I have to help him to lie low, and in the meantime get him some things that don't look too new.'

"The woman, for whom like most Irish the words 'Fenian' and 'police' were magic, became all smiles, and let me fill a valise with clothes at my own price. As I paid her she said, "'God bless you! May you have good luck and get off safe to America!'

"As I hurried away from the market I suddenly remembered I'd left a scarf with my initials embroidered on it back at the Cathedral Hotel. Cursing my forgetfulness, I hurried back. Too late! The place was already being watched by a young man leaning on a stick. No doubt the discovery of the scarf, my late arrival, early departure, and my meagre baggage had alerted the hotel and prompted someone there to notify the police. The best place to make for now was the station.

"Presenting myself at the ticket office, I adopted a new role. *'Parlez-vous Francais, monsieur?'*

"'No.'

"That wasn't a good start. I put on a fractured accent and somehow managed to buy a ticket for Drogheda. But as the train approached two men arrived at the station, began an excited conversation with the stationmaster, and all the time kept looking at me. I saw the ticket salesman lean across his counter and heard him say, 'He's a Frenchman.' I'm sure I was saved when he told them I'd bought a ticket to a way station only. A long time later I was to discover that on that day and the preceding day the Irish police arrested 12 men in the belief that they were me.

"The two men seemed satisfied with the railwaymen's explanations, and I got into the train. There were two farmers in my compartment, and the more sober one of the two had apparently just finished reading a newspaper article to his companion on the Great Bank Forgery. He turned to me and asked me if I had read the story.

"'Excuse, please, I French, not much understand.'

"'Well, then, I'll read it to you, sir.' He read out a fairly wild account of our lives as reported in a Dublin newspaper, then said: 'You being a Frenchman probably don't understand our great bank, but I can tell you those Yankees did a clever thing when they had a go at that institution. The fellow who's penned up here in Ireland can't escape, of course, in fact, some of the newspapers say he's already been arrested. I'm sorry if that's true, because you can't help thinking that clever rascals like that ought to get off.'

"His companion, who had been looking over his shoulder, said, 'There's a description of the one they reckon is in Ireland.' He read out a fair general outline of my appearance which fortunately he was completely unable to relate to me. Feeling more and more confident, I explained in broken French that owing to my ignorance of the language I had bought the wrong ticket; since we were all getting off at Drogheda would they mind buying me a ticket to Belfast? They were delighted to help, of course.

"I got to Belfast with no further incident and still speaking in fractured French bought a ticket for Glasgow from the purser on board the night steamer. As I went into the washroom I heard steps descending the cabin stairway and a voice said: 'Purser, a cab just brought a man from the Dublin train. Where is he?'

"'You mean the Frenchman?'

"I put on my silk hat and stood before the mirror in the best French pose I could muster. Two detectives stepped into my cabin, looked me over, then bade me *'Bonne nuit.'* And it was a good night, too. Exhausted, I dropped on the cabin bed and didn't wake until the steamer was coming into Glasgow."

Poor George! In due course he left Glasgow for

Edinburgh from where he tried repeatedly to board a ship, but everywhere was being watched. His lodgings in Cumberland Street. Edinburgh, were eventually discovered by a private detective named James McKelvie.

On 2nd April McKelvie watched George leave the lodgings, do a few small errands, and look suspiciously around him. McKelvie watched him stop at the door of a baker's shop, here, suddenly alarmed, he bolted round a corner. Then McKelvie decided to pursue him.

The chase led over stone walls and church railings, and ended in Duncan Street, Stockbridge.

George was panting for breath, and bleeding profusely from a cut in his leg which had happened during the chase, but he jabbed a stick he was carrying at his pursuer. McKelvie retaliated by producing a baton from inside his coat and shouting, "Sir, behave like a gentleman and not like a coward." Apparently thinking George must be a freemason, he held out his hand and added cryptically: "Come, be a brother." When George, who wasn't a freemason, extended his hand, McKelvie seized it and pinioned him. He called a cab and George was taken to a solicitor's office, where he was told he was wanted for forgery on the Bank of England.

George's reply was all gobbledegook. He told the solicitors in fractured French that he wasn't a Fenian.

"We know that," McKelvie replied. "Why did you run away from me?"

Again in fractured French George replied that he was prone to acts of giddiness which always made him want to run.

"What's your name?" McKelvie asked, who had got hold of some bandages by this time and was binding up George's cut leg.

"You may call me James if you like."

George was trying to make bricks without straw, and the bricks were crumbling around him. When the police arrived they confidently arrested him as George Bidwell. He was arraigned before a Scottish court and on a prosecution application was transferred to London, where he was taken to Newgate prison to await trial.

On their way south, his detective escort regaled him with their version of the chase after him. They had arrived in Cork three hours after he'd left; they traced the cab across the bridge and the shop where he got the boy to go for it. The woman owner of the shop was very voluble about him, describing his bag and scarf. But there was no trail to follow, so they telegraphed instructions to police within 50 miles to keep a look-out for him.

The next clue came from the carman returning at around 11 p.m. as drunk as a soldier on leave. They stuck this poor fellow's head under a cold-water tap until he was half drowned, and got him sober enough to say where he had left George. But he swore George was a priest. When the detectives roared with laughter the cabman said, "Ye may twist me head an' dhroun me intirely, but I wull niver spake another wurrud about the jintelman at all, at all." And he didn't, either.

The detectives took a carriage to the wayside inn, and got the old woman out of bed at midnight. After interrogating her and the boy who carried George's bag, they reckoned he had a six-hour start on them and intended taking the branch line at Fermoy for Dublin. At Fermoy they lost the trail. By telegraphing all the local police stations they discovered he had taken the opposite direction – a dispatch arrived from Lismore saying that a man had arrived on the last train, stayed at the Lismore Hotel, and left without paying his bill.

They guessed rightly he would make for Clonmel, found the hostler, who tore his hair when he was told he had let a £5,000 reward slip through his fingers. They met the cab he sent back from the country store. At Clonmel a police inspector told them he had sent a constable after a man who had hired a car to go to Caher – this was one of the men from whom George had escaped by dodging into the ruined cottage. They saw the

Clonmel mail car, but it had no one in it except the driver.

The constable from Clonmel told the detectives that George must have had a friend hiding him in the fort. He took them to see it, but as soon as they saw the ruined cottages they asked the constable if he'd searched them.

"No," he replied. "You can see they would be no place to hide, all open to the sky, and with no windows or doors."

One of the detectives borrowed the constable's lamp and flashed it around the place where George had been cowering a few hours earlier.

"You must be some kind of a fool," he said to the constable. "This is the only place he could have been hiding."

They gave Caher a complete turning over, but the only place where they could get any information was at Maloy's. Mrs. Maloy said a man had come in at dinnertime, saying he was an American seeing people in their homes; the Maloys had nothing further to add beyond that George had left.

The next clue was finding George's scarf at the Cathedral Hotel, Dublin, but after that the trail again went cold. Some weeks were to pass before the new, and final, sighting in Edinburgh.

11

A CIVIL WAR TO ADD TO MY PROBLEMS

As soon as I arrived in Paris I joined my fiancée Jane who was staying with her parents at the Hotel St. James, Rue Saint-Honoré. For the next few days we dined at Versailles and at Fontainebleau, and travelled around the city in my four-in-hand coach, the young dude and his bride-to-be on pleasure bent. One morning I opened my eyes and my first thought was, it will be hit or miss at the Bank of England within the next sixty minutes. We were due to drive out of the city for a day, and as I left I had a chilling feeling that before sunset I might be obliged to leave Paris permanently and in something of a hurry.

We were at dinner that evening when my valet, Nunn, came in and gave me a telegram. It said:

"All well. Bought and shipped forty bales."

That meant the first lot for $40,000 had gone through safely. Next day I received $25,000 in U. S. bonds from George in London, my first share of the proceeds. I sold the bonds in Paris, and was paid in French francs.

The day before I was to be married, I had a telegram from Mac and George to meet them in Calais. I arrived at midnight, just before the Dover steamer got in. Mac put a small but heavy bag in my hands filled with £4,000 in sovereigns, bonds and paper money. That was just for starters, for we went to a hotel where they then counted out $100,000 in gold, bonds and French francs.

We had only an hour to talk before their return boat. We all shook hands warmly, they to return to continue plundering the Bank, and I, blissfully unaware that I would never see them as free men again for many years to come, to my wedding. At 4 p.m. that afternoon I was married at the American Embassy.

I made sure that all those who came to the wedding and inquired where we were off to for our honeymoon understood that it was to America via Le Havre. In fact, I'd bought a ticket to Bayonne, another to Madrid, and a third to Burgos, all from different agencies. My plan was to get to Cadiz and from there to take the steamer *El Rey Felipe* to Mexico ten days after we were married.

Like all English people my wife knew little about geography. Her notion of America was so hazy that she could see nothing untoward about going there via a Spanish port; after all, Columbus had gone that way, so why shouldn't we?

So we slipped out by train to Bayonne, and from there crossed the Bidassoa, on the border between France and Spain. It is difficult enough for an American to imagine that so slight a thing as a mountain chain can divide completely different peoples, even more difficult to understand that for nearly all time the inhabitants of the Spanish mountains have been more or less opposed to the people of the Spanish plains. This was the crazy situation we were headed straight into. In 1872 and 1873 the Carlists under their leader Don Carlos held the mountains and were fighting for their territory – the possibility of my way being blocked by them had never remotely entered my calculations.

The railway from Bayonne to Madrid is owned in Paris and it seemed that the directors were paying 100,000 francs' blackmail to Don Carlos, or ostensibly to him but in reality to several marauding bands who plundered under the name of fighting for the Don, on the understanding that they would leave the railway alone. The greedy and inartistic discontented, who probably didn't think they were getting enough of the cash, had decided to hold up the railway and stop all trains; unfortunately for us, ours was the first one they chose. As we entered the magnificent gorges of the Pyrenees three or four musket shots rang out. The train came to a shuddering stop, and looking out of the window we saw ourselves surrounded by armed men, a laughable array of brigands all trying to maintain the grave Spanish exterior.

They made us get out of the train, and looking around at my fellow-travellers I decided to take charge. Using a priest among us as interpreter, I made it clear to the brigands that I was an English duke travelling with his duchess, and the wrath of England would descend upon them if we were harmed in any way.

"Sir," replied their chief, "we are soldiers, not robbers."

"I am very glad to hear it. Are we supposed to be prisoners?"

"No, but we shall be obliged to detain you for a few days." He jerked his thumb over his shoulder. "There is an inn three miles away, where your wife can take shelter."

As soon as Jane was settled I set off riding mule-back five miles to see the local Carlist commander, who promised to send me the next day a pass through the lines, going north or south. I got him to include all my fellow-passengers, because I was worried about a Portuguese family on the train who had tickets for South America via Lisbon. The head of their family was weak and ill, and clearly his condition would be aggravated by this sort of delay.

When the pass came through we were advised to go south and get to a little town about 30 miles away from where trains left frequently for Madrid. I bought three old bullock carts, with eight bullocks and four mules, and hired 13 Spanish porters. I put all the women and the sick Portuguese in one cart, and all the luggage in the other two, and we set off, with myself and my valet Nunn trudging alongside the cart with the women.

At first the road was good, then it began to wind upwards, always upwards, into snow. In the mid-afternoon the sky darkened and down came more snow. We stopped to rest the bullocks and I got out some brandy and blankets. When we pressed on it was already dark, and two hours later our Spaniards – they were a bunch of beauties, I must say – said they could go no farther.

After an angry scene they agreed that we should send a party ahead led by me with some of the Spaniards and with the cart containing the women; Nunn would stay behind with the luggage carts, and, incidentally, a revolver that I had given him. So it was that an hour and a half later my forward party reached a wretched mountain inn, where at least we got a supper of Spanish beans for the women. A bed was made up on the floor and they were all soon sound asleep. Then I started back through the snow to rescue Nunn and the other Spaniards.

The journey back through the deepening snow to Nunn, and then back to the mountain inn, had me on my knees, but I was happy because I knew my wife was safe. That night Nunn and I slept on the hay in the inn's stable, and we awoke next morning to a howling blizzard. We were trapped.

It was now Thursday, the fourth day since we had left Paris, and I had no idea what was happening in London – I might just as well have been on a desert island. Our steamer was due to sail from Cadiz on Monday, and if I missed it anything might happen.

Our host made the best of things by decapitating any chickens that happened to be around, so that we had chicken, roasted by the versatile Nunn, for breakfast, lunch and dinner. There was plenty of wine in the place, and the Spaniards, who had reason to be merry for I was paying them a dollar a day, danced for our entertainment. All this would have been wonderfully idyllic had I not got a boat to catch. Fortunately, the storm cleared just after midnight, and although the Spaniards objected bitterly, and played out a whole pantomime of reasons for not moving, next morning we were on our way again.

With my wife leading the way on a mule, the rest of us trudged for hour after hour through the snow. In the mid-afternoon we came across some Carlist officers, one of whom was a young Englishman, and A.D.C. on Don Carlos's staff. He turned out to be a genial fellow.

"There's no chance of our side winning," he confided to me. "I'm only in it for the fun of the thing, and a chance to see some fighting."

"Have you seen any action yet?" I asked him.

"A few skirmishes, but not enough. Anyway, for the moment I think I'd better escort you through the lines."

I think his chief reason for so doing was that he was pleased to see an English lady in the person of my wife. At any rate he was a brave and brilliant fellow, just what we needed. He bullied my muleteers up and down dale, and didn't hesitate to use his whip on them. He told us we had 20 miles to cover to reach a little town on the railway south of the Pyrenees, and with two lanterns and a number of torches we must have looked a picturesque caravan. The young English officer rode beside the first cart, talking with my wife, while I brought up the rear.

Presently we rode through a camp, where the English officer turned out the guard to greet us. A number of officers – French, English, Austrian – came by to chat to us along the snow-lined path. Our torches cast fantastic shadows that seemed to reach to the forest-covered mountain, dark and frowning, though snow lay every-where, and all this made a picture I will never forget.

A mile more and our escort had to leave us, but the town was now in full view. The station was fortified and full of soldiers, but there was room for us to make beds and get settled down for the night. My party seemed to sleep well – for me, two hours was enough.

The weather continued very cold, and when the train

of just three cars, one for baggage and the other two for passengers, arrived, there were no heating arrangements, and we shivered at the thought of an all-day ride without fire or heat across the windy plain.

I determined to have a compartment to ourselves, for my wife and I had not had a moment's privacy since our train was ambushed. So we fixed up a bed on the compartment floor for our sick Portuguese, and put his family in to look after him. When the train left Jane and I found ourselves alone, much to our satisfaction. I had telegraphed ahead to Burgos to have hot-water cases, then the only method of heating trains in Europe, ready on our arrival.

At Burgos we had to change to the train from Santander, going south, and there was a two-hour wait. There was also some startling news for us to think about. Nothing less than a revolution had occurred in Madrid. The lately elected King Amadeo had quit and a republic proclaimed with Castelar at its head.

Our ship was due to leave Cadiz on Monday, and it was now 3 p.m. on Friday. I began to see more and more what a fool I was to let myself be caught at such a time in such a country. When the train finally arrived and we set out for Madrid I made some calculations. We would be in Madrid next morning. From there to Cadiz there was only one through train a day, seven days a week, but as it ran at only fifteen miles an hour and was always late, I needed to allow 24 hours for the journey. That would take us until Sunday morning, still allowing a seemingly safe margin for the unforeseen.

The unforeseen was soon to surface. At Avila, about 150 miles from Madrid, we learned that martial law had been proclaimed and that the government had seized the railways to transport troops. Furious, I piled our baggage out of the train and once more set up camp on the station floor, while a terrific din went on around us for all the rest of the night.

Next morning I telegraphed Castelar and the Minister

of War that I was an Englishman, that I had important business in Madrid and must not be detained in Avila. I demanded a special train. I also sent a telegram to Hernandez, president of the railway in Paris, offering 5,000 francs for a special train, and another to the superintendent in Madrid repeating the offer, adding the same sum for himself if he expedited the train, plus the same sum again if it was necessary to bribe the military authorities.

All this began slowly to have some effect. Various messages came down the line, the last one, at midday, followed by an engine and car. The soldiers and locals flocked around as we boarded; doubtless the little station had never seen such important passengers. A special train was an unheard-of thing in Spain, if only because no particle of matter between a Spaniard's chin and his sombrero can conceive that anything born of woman could be insane enough to be in a hurry. The engine blew its whistle, then the telegraph operator dashed out with an order for our train to await the arrival of the train from Madrid.

I stormed and raved. I sent message after message down the wire. The only response I could get was that the delay was temporary. But my heart was beginning to fill with bitterness, for I saw the precious hours slipping away, and with them my chance of taking the Sunday morning train so as to catch the Cadiz ship. If I missed that, I reckoned, I would be ruined.

Jane, all unaware of my secret fears, chatted away to all and sundry, telling everyone she was the happiest of women. Why should she care about revolutions and delays when she was with me! The sun began to go down and the shadows fell.

At 6 p.m. a message came to have everything ready to pull out for Madrid at 7. But no order came. The hours dragged on while I sensed fate closing her hand on me.

Towards midnight the operator rushed out of his office, shouted to the driver, and in a moment we were off. I had given the driver a tip, and as he put on speed hope slowly ebbed back through me. At the Escurial, 70 miles from Madrid, we were run into a side line to clear the track for a train going north. For two miserable hours we waited, and no train. Just as the eastern skies grew grey we started again.

At the next stop there was just time for me to telegraph the authorities at Madrid to hold the train going south to Cadiz until my arrival, offering $100 a hour for every hour I delayed it. I need not have bothered. Madrid is situated on a high sandy plain, storm-swept in winter, and we had a wheezy engine. It did only four more miles before it broke down, and then I gave up the struggle.

So here I was at last in Madrid nine hours too late for the Cadiz train. The only way out now was by a French steamer *Martinique* sailing from St. Nazaire, on the French west coast, for Veracruz, Mexico, which would stop at Santander for mail and passengers the following Saturday. It meant retracing our steps through Avila to Burgos, and changing there for Santander, a prima facie case of lunacy for a man in my position, but there was simply no alternative.

We said our last good-byes to the Portuguese family with their sick relative and despite their gratitude I was in truth happy to see them go. They had been an encumbrance, and a serious expense, albeit that all expenses were being paid for by the Bank of England. The good news I discovered before leaving Madrid came from a visit to the British Embassy, where not one of the London newspapers reported anything untoward from the City. At least, I thought, the kind Old Lady of Threadneedle Street is continuing to shell out sovereigns by the tens of thousands to me.

We spent that weekend sight-seeing in Madrid, and on Tuesday set off for Santander, arriving after a day and a night of travelling. Three more days of enforced idleness brought us to Saturday, and no *Martinique*. She came in 24 hours late on Sunday, and I never saw a happier sight, nor felt a greater thrill when, with my servant Nunn, my wife and myself safely aboard, she put out to sea again.

At last I could begin to re-examine my plans for the new life I was about to embark upon. The *Martinique* was to call at St. Thomas to take on coal after 18 days at sea; from there, after a stop of two or three days, she would proceed for another 24 hours to Havana in Cuba, staying for one day before sailing on to Veracruz.

It was my intention to leave the ship at Veracruz and set out across country to Mexico City. Although I never imagined pursuit beyond New York, once in Mexico I would be safe from all danger. To be in that country was akin to being in the middle of darkest Africa, there was no extradition treaty, no railways, and no telegraph, and I had plenty of cash to buy an estate near the capital and settle down for two or three years.

And so it all seemed to work out. We did the tourist thing in St. Thomas, and set off for Havana. As we sailed along the Cuban coast I thought I had never seen such an enchanting island. As soon as we were ashore both Jane and I were convinced that a day simply wasn't enough for so fine a place. I told the shipping agent that we would stay on there because we liked it so much, and take the next steamer in a month's time for Veracruz. When I think back about that decision I reckon I must have needed my head examined.

What attracted us to Cuba? Probably its uniqueness. Slavery was rife. On our occasional visits to the sugar plantations it was clear that brutality was part of the order of things. The sun shone every day and the scenery remained a luxuriant green. The house we rented had magnificent views of the Gulf of Mexico, and the rental included ten slaves and excellent horses. A nice if slightly gossipy group of Americans wintered regularly there, and we soon got to know quite a few of them, all enchanted with the accent of my English wife.

I got to know, too, General Torbert, the American Consul, who introduced me to the Spanish police chief, Colonel Moreno de Vascos. I took the Colonel out to dinner on several occasions, until I was confident that if any telegrams came about me he would bring them to me for an explanation, and would probably give me plenty of time to depart from the island if I suddenly had to.

None of my friends in London had any idea where I was, of course. I kept an eye on the New York papers arriving in Havana every day, but their silence indicated that Mac, George and Noyes were having amazing success.

Content with my wealth and the cards fortune had dealt me, I settled back to enjoy Cuba; I thought I deserved every minute of the rest. After a few weeks of this Nunn rode up one day from a visit to Havana and handed me the *New York Herald*. I went on talking to Jane as I opened it and the headlines leapt out at me.

AMAZING FRAUD UPON THE BANK OF ENGLAND!

MILLIONS LOST!

GREAT EXCITEMENT IN LONDON!

£5,000 REWARD FOR THE ARREST OF THE AMERICAN PERPETRATOR, F. A. WARREN.

And under this was the following dispatch;
London, Feb. 14, 1873.
An amazing fraud has been perpetrated upon the Bank of England by a young American who gave the name of Frederick Albert Warren. The loss of the bank is reported to be from three to ten millions, and it is rumored that many London banks have been victimized to enormous amounts. The greatest excitement prevails in the city, and the forgery,

for such it is, is the one topic of conversation on the Exchange and in the street. The police are completely at fault, although a young man named Noyes, who was Warren's clerk, has been arrested, but it is believed that he is a dupe.

The bank has offered a reward of £5,000 for information leading to the arrest of Warren or any confederate.

12

"MR. BIDWELL, YOU ARE MY PRISONER!"

I took a long walk along the beach to think things over. My first concern was for Noyes, who should never have been arrested if the right precautions had been taken. All sorts of ideas rushed through my mind. First, he would never betray us. Second, his arrest could only be for a brief period. Third, my right name would never come out. Fourth, Mac and George couldn't conceivably be implicated ... This, of course, is how one's mind works when one is alone and thousands of miles from the scene of the action.

I came back along the beach with my plans outlined. I would remain quietly where I was for a fortnight longer, then take ship to Veracruz, and from there proceed to Mexico City and my real-estate plan. No one knew I was in Cuba and as long as my name didn't come out I was as safe here as in the desert. *Courage, mon brave!* There was no need even to change my life-style on the island.

Day after day the story continued to make front-page news, and before long it was the talk of our gossipy little ex-pat community. My wife came home from cocktails one day and began telling me about some daring fellow-countryman of mine "who had the audacity to rob the Bank of England" and "who ought to have a whipping". When the island's Americans began discussing with me who this fellow Warren could possibly be I was mighty pleased to learn that the next ship for Veracruz called by in a few days' time, and I determined to sail on her. But fate was to take another unexpected twist.

One of my first and firmest friends in Cuba was a wealthy young countryman of mine named Gray. He had a friend named Senor Andrez, a Cuban planter with a vast coffee plantation in the Isla de Pinos, the largest island off the south coast of Cuba in the Caribbean Sea. When Andrez invited Gray to spend a week on his plantation Gray insisted upon taking me along as one of his party.

I had met Andrez and liked him, and he too added his weight to the invitation to the point where it would have been churlish to refuse. But it also meant that I would miss the next sailing to Veracruz.

Did it matter, I asked myself. No one knew who I was. Why shouldn't I have some fun? My wife did not relish my going, and her view of it added to my misgivings, but in the end the warmth of friendship proved irresistible, and I decided to go, convinced that the affair in London was shrouded in so dense a fog that the detectives on the case would never discover the identity of any of us.

The truth was far different. As I set out on my jaunt to the Isla de Pinos the Pinkerton detective force in London had cracked the whole plot, to the extent that one of their senior men, Captain John Curtin, in New York, had reported that whenever F. A. Warren was discovered he would prove to be none other than Austin Bidwell.

Even so, I decided to take some precautions. Before leaving on the trip I instructed Nunn to leave Havana secretly after telling his mistress that I had ordered him to go to Matanzas, forty miles away. He was to bring all the New York newspapers, meet me at Caijo and let no one know his destination.

If meantime anything unusual happened he was to leave at once for Caijo, hire a boat and crew and come after me. I reckoned that during my stay in the Isla de Pinos I would be out of reach of the outside world, but if when Nunn arrived I saw any signs of danger I wouldn't return to Havana, but would hire a boat and provisions and sail to some port in Central America, from where I would send my servant back to collect my wife. Nunn, fortunately, was one of those rare men who knew how to accept orders without self-questionings.

In Havana we regarded Don Andrez as a good fellow, but upon the arrival of our party of four – myself, Gray and two others – at San Felipe he had grown into a man of importance. At Caijo he had mushroomed into a person of distinction, and by the time we arrived at the Isla de Pinos he was a local Caesar.

We went from San Felipe to Caijo with pack-horses, crossing Cuba at its narrowest part, and travelling through dense tropical vegetation. There was much evidence of looting and burning along the fertile coastal belt, caused, we learned, by insurgents landing only a few weeks earlier from the eastern province of Santiago de Cuba and creating much havoc with cries of "Free Cuba and death to the Spaniard!" They had blotted out a town, then marched into the heart of the country, burning homes, killing whites, and calling on slaves to join them.

The final battle was joined at the village of San Marcos, where they were all butchered by the loyal soldiers, and their mutilated bodies burned in the open air. The ashes of these fires were still evident as we passed by, and we stopped and contemplated them in silence for some minutes.

Don Andrez met us at Caijo, where he had a house; we were served at once with black coffee and thin, fried rice cakes. The air was delightful and following the custom of the country we slept in grass-woven hammocks, slung under the roof in front of the house, without undressing.

Next morning Gray and I made for the beach early

and dived into the brilliant blue-green water; then our party set out on an open-decked cargo boat from Caijo for San José, in the Isla de Pinos, 70 miles across the water and on the west coast of the island. San José was one of the half-dozen coffee plantations belonging to our host, and everything on our ship – men, women, children slaves, two trained pigs, dogs, turtles, fighting cocks and a good-sized snake that answered to the name of Jacko – belonged to our host, including the ship itself.

The week that followed was one I will not easily forget. We went shark-fishing every day, and watched the Cubans indulge themselves with their fighting cocks. We swam, ate and drank like kings, and at the end of the week I had sadly to insist that I must return to Havana to catch up on my business interests. Gray was to stay on for another week, so I set off alone, and a few hours later arrived back at Caijo, where Nunn was waiting for me on the beach with the papers.

I was amazed to see that the story was still front-page news, and that all the papers were speculating about the identity of F. A. Warren. I had a sudden overwhelming desire to get out of Cuba and start living under another name, taking my wife into my confidence somewhere along the line. It had to be Mexico, and it had better be soon.

Back in Havana it was evident that nothing was yet known. There was a steamer in the harbour due to sail to Mexico in two days, but my wife had sent out dinner invitations for that very same day for twenty people, so we were obliged to stay. Another ship was leaving on Saturday for Veracruz, and that would have to suffice.

I bit my lip at this unforeseen delay, but as our guests began to arrive and in the knowledge that we would be on our way in another 48 hours, I relaxed and decided to enjoy myself. As we sat down the long windows were open and the warm breeze from the gulf below was wafting pleasantly through the room.

We had finished the dessert and were just awaiting the

coffee service when we all stopped talking at once – from the veranda came the noise of hurrying feet quite out of character with our leisurely dinner party. All eyes turned to the open door leading to the hall, from which we could now see a dozen men suddenly crowding in, civilians and soldiers jostling my staff. I pushed back my chair determined to tackle these intruders, but before I could move more than two steps one of the party detached himself and came straight round the table towards me. His words made my blood freeze.

"Mr. Austin Bidwell, I am Captain John Curtin of the Pinkerton detective force. I have a warrant for your arrest on a charge of forgery on the Bank of England. The warrant is signed by the Captain-General of Cuba, and you are my prisoner."

My first thought was for my wife. I shall never forget the look on her face. She was deathly white.

"There appears to be some unhappy mistake," I said, recollecting myself. "I am sorry to ask everyone to leave so suddenly, but I am sure I will be able to explain everything tomorrow."

As my unfortunate guests hurried away, mumbling to themselves, I took in the scene. There were five soldiers, and they already had Nunn under arrest. Behind the dining room was a large sitting-room, to where I now led Captain Curtin.

"Would you like a glass of wine?" I asked him.

"Certainly. But I never drink anything but Clicquot."

Luckily, we had some. A servant brought the bottle and two glasses. Could this parvenu policeman be bribed, I wondered. If not, I would have to shoot him, for there was a loaded revolver in the drawer at my elbow. As he sniffed the Clicquot I pointed to a trunk and said: "There is $50,000 in there. Sit where you are for ten minutes, give no alarm, and you can have it."

Curtin drained his glass before answering. Then, setting it back on the table, he said, "Why, Mr. Bidwell, that's $5,000 a minute."

"A bargain for you, Curtin."

"And you can keep it, Bidwell."

Seeing me move my arm, he leapt to his feet, but he was too late. The revolver was in my hand. I fired point-blank and he went down in a crumpled heap.

I made for the window as one of Curtin's subordinates, revolver in hand, sprang from the outer darkness. My wife rushed in from the dining-room. Curtin pulled himself up from the floor; suddenly I was surrounded and my hands were bound behind my back.

My bullet had struck Curtin in one rib, breaking it before glancing off. He seemed to take it good-naturedly, and rode in the carriage that took me to a hotel, where I was to sleep with three soldiers as room-mates. Early next morning my friend the chief of police, Colonel de Vascos, called, all indignant and angry that I should have to suffer such discourtesy.

"Let him go at once!" he commanded Curtin. For answer Curtin waved a packet of papers which appeared to be orders from the State Department in Washington. No one could override them, he declared stubbornly.

At midday I was transferred to the police barracks, and put under close guard in a police lieutenant's room. There I languished through the rest of the day and the night, and the next morning the police lieutenant came in to see me and told me that they had a cable from New York, and the story of my arrest was front-page news all over America. There was only one thing for it now, I decided – I had to escape while I was still being held in the police barracks.

Curtin guessed my intentions. He spent hours protesting that I should be held in prison, but Colonel Vascos wouldn't hear of it. Nunn was released and came to see me regularly; I took him into my confidence and told him I was going to escape.

I had every reason to give thanks for Spanish law. Curtin tried in vain to seize my effects; instead, Vascos willingly arranged for two of my trunks to be brought to me unopened. I had $80,000 in cash and bonds, besides many valuables, in them, and I stowed as much of the cash as I could in my clothes. Already I was forming a vague idea of escaping to the Western Province, where the native Cubans, mulattos and Negro ex-slaves were in full rebellion. I figured on joining the insurgents for a year, where the army wouldn't dare to pursue me, then somehow getting across the narrow stretch of water between Cape San Antonio and the mainland of South America.

My wife too had to be taken into my confidence. She was totally bewildered and confused by the events, and not in a fit state to agree to anything. But at last I persuaded her that she must leave Havana as soon as she heard that I was free, cross to Key West, wait a month there, telegraph my sister to meet her in New York, and go to live with her there until I was able to meet up with her again.

Nunn had brought me maps of the island and arms, all that remained now was to escape. That was much easier than it might seem. I had habitually given the guards a bottle of brandy and a box of cigars every second day of my incarceration, so I was thought to be a likeable fellow. My room was on the second floor of the barracks, but I was given free access to all the second-floor rooms, followed more or less by a guard. There was just one room leading to an open window facing the street, but the door was kept locked. A few dollars sufficed to ensure that one of the guards would leave it unlocked, with the key inside, at 10 o'clock on the night of 20th March.

Early that evening Nunn came with my supper, a revolver and an ammunition belt. He would be in the street below the window from where I was to make my jump at 10 p.m., and he would stop anyone who tried to stop me, shooting them if necessary. At 7 p.m. he left. I gave the guard and three or four idle soldiers liberal doses of brandy, and an hour later the American

Consul-General Torbet, who was convinced of my innocence, came in to smoke a cigar and have a chat. He stayed until ten minutes to ten, leaving me just enough time to prepare myself. I began my walkabout along the corridors of the second floor, got out of sight of the slow-moving guard for four or five seconds and slipped through the unlocked door, locking it behind me.

Outside the window there was a little balcony. I climbed over the railing and hung suspended for an instant from the bottom. A crowd gathered below in a circle as I dropped easily to the ground, where the waiting Nunn clapped a large straw hat on my head. This strange incident didn't seem to arouse anyone's curiosity and in a moment we were lost in the crowd.

We slipped into a house, which Nunn had arranged as a stopping-place with the owner, and he and I both donned a set of bushy whiskers. Then we left by the back door where a cab was waiting, and arrived at the station just in time to catch the 10.30 train.

Everything had gone just as I'd planned, and now a great wave of happiness was sweeping over me. I had been a prisoner for the best part of a week, and I knew that, shut away from Nature's sights and sounds I made a bad captive. That brief deprivation had sharpened all my senses and made me cherish liberty as never before. Now I almost forgot I was a fugitive. Luckily, the Spaniard is not a suspicious animal and no notice was taken of us as we bumped slowly southward through the tropic night towards Guisa, 20 miles from Caijo.

Seven o'clock next morning brought us to Guisa, where we procured horses and set out for Caijo. We had police passports and gun permits in the names of Parish and Ellis, and I had a watch, several valuable diamonds, a revolver and a gun. Nunn carried a canvas bag containing among other things 250 excellent cigars, tobacco, matches, and 300 cartridges. We had good maps of the island and current charts of the Gulf of Mantabano. But armed as we were we knew that if we were picked up by the Spanish police anywhere near the rebel border our passports wouldn't hold good, and it would probably mean death.

At Caijo we bought some provisions and our passports were demanded by a little yellow monkey of a sergeant. I didn't like having our passports scrutinised, and decided to try and avoid any more of it.

The way forward now was either by sea or by land, and both ways were perilous. Two miles outside Caijo, on the edge of the jungle, I decided to send Nunn back to Havana and to go it alone. He wasn't happy, but I insisted. He was a man of exceptional courage and loyalty. We sat down in the vegetation for our last talk and smoked cigars. I gave him the gun and kept two revolvers, with 300 cartridges. I also took two bottles of water, a hundred cigars, four pounds of dried beef and a loaf of bread.

I wore the watch round my neck held by a string, and in my pockets I had $700 in gold and $5,000 in Spanish bank notes, plus $10,000 in bonds. I told Nunn to tell my wife Jane I would limit my stay with the rebels to no more than a year. He was to send for his wife to join him in New York, and my wife would take them both into service. When we parted it was not as master and servant, but as friends.

Under cover of night I set out west towards Pinar del Rio and the rebel camps, while Nunn went the other way, eastwards back to Caijo. At this time everything was very primitive in Cuba. The whites and free people lived in huts or cabins and slept in hammocks under roofs open on two sides. Everyone went to bed soon after sunset, so that it was safest to travel at night, making sure to circumvent the occasional detached post of soldiers.

I started out at a quick pace, alert and confident. The moon had gone down, but the Caribbean Sea was lovely by starlight. Watching the phosphorescent ripples on the water on one side of me and listening to the night noises in the jungle on the other side, I found I was almost beginning to enjoy my jaunt. Now and then I jumped with fright at some spook, any rock, stump or bush which to my suspicious eye might be a Spanish sentry. Then I sought the shelter of the jungle and spent seemingly ages scanning the darkness for some kind of movement. For the most part, though, I trudged along in the balmy June night, loaded with my two bottles of water and my revolvers and cartridges.

At midnight I sat down for half an hour and ate a meal of bread and dried beef, followed by an excellent Havana. At 4 a.m. the sky put on a ragged edge of grey in the east, and feeling pretty well satisfied with my progress I began to look for a place to hide during the daytime.

While I searched, the precariousness of my position became more and more evident. Daylight revealed a well-travelled road a few hundred yards inland from the beach, and between the road and the beach, and extending as far as the eye could see into the jungle was a swamp. The way ahead was thus impassable, unless I chose the road, and the danger of that was evidenced when, squatting down in the jungle to watch it, I counted 30 people passing by, soldiers, *guardia civil* and Negroes.

As the sun passed overhead I conceived a plan. I spent the rest of the day fashioning a raft from jungle wood and creepers, determined now to go ahead as far as possible by sea, which in itself was perilous enough, for the seas around Cuba are shark-infested. Toiling away throughout all that afternoon under cover of the dense undergrowth, I kept myself amused by thinking what a strange fate had fallen upon F. A. Warren, international fraudster with an account at the Bank of England.

13

A FUGITIVE IN THE JUNGLE

Night fell at last. As the moon went down I wasn't impatient, for the beauty of the scene effaced the danger of my position, casting a charm over my spirit and soothing both eye and mind.

I had noticed a bridge crossing the neck of the swamp, and had debated long enough with myself to recognise that the least dangerous way of getting past the swamp was to follow the line of the bridge on my raft, risking the danger of being seen. That was a real danger, too. On the far side of the bridge there were houses resting against it forming a street, a gauntlet which I would eventually have to run.

At midnight I carried my raft down to the edge of the water, then had a sudden change of mind. The bridge had no protection along the side save a simple length of timber. I decided it would be marginally safer to leave my raft there in the water in case of emergency, and creep along the length of timber as close as I could get to the houses.

I had gone more than half-way when I stopped, peered through the gloom and listened. I couldn't hear a thing, so I straightened up painfully, and walked on half a dozen paces. Suddenly I heard a match strike, and a waxen flame revealed two soldiers sitting on a bench in a guardhouse porch less than three metres away. One of them had struck the match to light a cigarette. The flame that betrayed them to me showed to them my form outlined against the bridge.

A shout of *"Quién va?"*, a rattle of accoutrements, and I had already turned and was flying back across the bridge. Two rifle shots missed me as I leapt on to my raft and, pushing it in front of me, waded out in the shallow water. Soon I began to swim, still pushing the raft ahead of me.

I was aware of all the commotion ashore. Two more shots were fired, and gun-flashes suggested a squad had turned out and had crossed the bridge after me. They would surely search the jungle, and in that case my fore-thought in constructing the raft had saved me.

Now, though, a new terror ran through me. When a large fish jumped only a metre or so from me I fancied I was surrounded by shoals of sharks. I saw myself being torn from limb to limb; instinctively I put my hand on my knife, but strength and courage were all gone and my nerveless hand couldn't even pull it from its scabbard. Half dazed, I waited for death, which I hoped when it came would be swift.

I was so absorbed with my own fear that I hadn't noticed how far I had come in the rear of the houses. When I did I made a rush for the shore and fell down weak and panting. Courage and confidence seeped slowly back and I started off again. I trudged on for another three hours, passing several salt-water inlets, but no fresh water to fill my now empty bottle.

At the first sign of day I slipped into the jungle and soon fell asleep. When I awoke it was nine o'clock and I was hungry and thirsty.

I set off through the tangled woods and after going about a mile I came to the road. Away to the west there were cultivated hills with people moving about them. The road ahead divided and both roads were well trav-elled. I guessed I was near the tobacco belt, which was cultivated along its entire length from the Gulf to the Caribbean Sea for a width of twenty miles, its western border touching the province of Pinar del Rio. Forty miles beyond that border the rebels held the town of San Cristoval.

I made up my mind that it would be safer to take the coast road to Rio de San Diego, then strike out from there to San Cristoval. Once past San Diego I would be well within the rebel lines, and could safely show myself. I reckoned it would take ten days, or rather nights, to get to San Diego, and five from there to the inland town of Passos, where I would most likely meet the rebel chiefs to whom I would declare myself a volunteer in the cause of Cuban liberty.

Food and water were the more immediate problems. I was hoping to find a crab to eat, but no such luck. I decided to start early on my journey that evening and try to get some food before the country people went to bed. When night fell I stepped out on to the road and cautiously started westward. There had to be a town or hamlet close by; I would watch until the shopkeeper was alone and buy as much as I could before disappearing into the night.

Soon I came to an isolated house. There were two women in the doorway. I strode up to them purposefully.

"Buenas noches, senoritas. Agua?"

They responded with alacrity and brought me a coconut shell brimming with water. It was vile stuff with an earthy taste, but I drank it at a gulp. Seeing me looking at some food on a table, the older woman handed me two roasted plantains and a rice cake. There was no time for more, for behind her I noticed a man inside the house and two others came round the back. I thanked the women and disappeared like a ghost into the night.

A mile ahead I came to a tumble-down roadhouse where a group of loud-voiced men who had evidently been indulging in the fiery *aguardiente* sold there were arguing fiercely. Like the Levite and priest, I passed by on the other side, giving the place a wide berth.

Later I came to a village of a dozen houses. Two uniformed men, evidently police or soldiers, were lounging in the only shop. Positioning myself in deep shadow, I sat down waiting for them to leave; eventually they were called away by a shrill female voice issuing from a nearby house. With my hand on the revolver in my outside pocket, I entered the shop.

The shopkeeper paid me no particular attention. I said, *"Buenas noches, senor;"* his response was indifferent. I paid for some cakes, bread, ham, and a bottle of pickles and some Spanish wine with a $10 Spanish banknote.

It seemed ages before I could find a safe place along the road to sit down and eat. This at last was the ruins of a house which thankfully lay by a stream of fresh water. For the next hour I was in Nirvana, indulging myself with a feast fit for the gods.

I struck out on the road leading to the beach and marched westwards, all the time fearful of running against some military post or patrol and constantly making long detours to avoid some suspicious object. Once I had a fright. Two men on horseback riding along the sandy road were almost on me before I saw or heard them, and I had only enough time to sink into the shadow as they passed almost within reach of my hand. When daylight broke I calculated I had made eight or ten miles, and curled up under cover to sleep.

The next night was uneventful, except for the fact that my provisions were fast disappearing and I had to eat lightly. I lay down to sleep in sight of the blue sea and awoke when the stars were out. I reckon I must have made 25 miles that night, but the indented coast meant that my progress in a straight direction couldn't have been more than half that distance. Just as first light was streaking the horizon I came out on to a wide inlet which ran deep into the land. I recognised it from the map as Puerto del Gato, and I knew then that I was in the province of Pinar del Rio and almost out of danger.

I went into the bush, scraped a few leaves together,

and lay down. But I was too excited to sleep. I felt I was close to my goal and had survived so many dangers. Once I was across the Puerto del Gato I would need only two more nights of marching to put me out of reach of the farthest Spanish pickets, far beyond pursuit. And just the knowledge of my presence in the rebel camp would be enough for my pursuers to give up the chase.

With the coming of daylight I took stock of my position. To the north the land was hilly, with houses dotted about in the distance and signs of animal life. Cautiously I searched the shore for a mile, hoping to find a boat to cross to the other shore of the inlet, but there was no such luck.

At nine o'clock I saw smoke off at sea; a small Spanish gunboat came rapidly up. Dropping anchor about a mile up the inlet, she sent a boat ashore. I went back into the woods again, ate a light lunch, and decided to have a nap. I didn't much like the appearance of the gunboat. It boded ill, besides being a manifestation of the power of my enemy.

Waking, I started on a cautious spying out of the land. Almost at once I was startled by a bugle ringing out some military call not far away; a moment later the gunboat replied with a gun, then steamed out to sea. Hiding in a thicket where I could see unseen, I watched.

First came the sound of voices, then a detail of armed men passed, escorting a wagon drawn by four mules. Several others passed during the hour of my watch. With cautious glances up and down the road, I slipped quietly across and crept for two hours through the jungle. Making my way to the side of the bay, I could see the military post was now behind me. There were white barracks and a wharf with people walking on it, and here the road and beach were one. This much discovered, I went a safe distance into the jungle and lay down to have a good sleep, feeling I would need all my energy and strength for the coming night.

I slept until dark and awoke refreshed, then ate some food and nearly finished my last bottle of water. I had sufficient food for only two more light meals. At nine o'clock I started cautiously out, walking in the shadow of the jungle as much as possible. I reckoned the head of the inlet was about ten miles away, and I expected to find a military post or at least a picket stationed there ...

Daylight once more. But now I was supremely happy, for the difficulties of getting round the wide inlet which had confronted me the night before had all been overcome. I was now in a densely wooded point on the western side of the bay. Between me and San Diego lay a wild no-man's land of fifty miles, two nights only of peril and uncertainty, and it was all straight going. As far as the coastline was concerned, I was now outside the Spanish lines.

As the sun rose fiery red above the horizon I lay down and slept at once. I woke at noon, hungry and with only a few morsels of food left. For the thousandth time I scanned my little map. Six miles to the north was the town of San Miguel. I had to go there to get food before going on to San Diego; there was no way I could make a two-day journey through that wilderness without eating.

That evening I set out for the little town and arrived around nine o'clock. The moonlight cast a deep shadow on one side of the single street, while the opposite side was almost like day. I stood in the deep shadow watching. The first building was evidently a police or military barracks. Five doors farther on was a shop, but the door was closed. I waited about ten minutes, then thinking that there could be no one there but the owner, I stepped out of the shadow into the moonlight. I crossed the street rapidly, put my hand on the shop door and went in.

Inside were about twenty soldiers, gossiping, smoking, gambling. All twenty pairs of eyes were turned upon me.

My heart began to thump, but I guessed that nothing

but consummate coolness could stop them questioning me. With an affectation of indifference I saluted and said, *"Buenos noches, senores."* They returned my salutation in a chorus, then all looked at each other, each waiting for the other to ask a question.

I stepped to the counter and asked for bread; two loaves were handed to me. I picked up some cakes and paid for them. From the door I turned and, putting all my dignity into a bow, said, *"Buenos noches, senores."* They all seemed held by a spell, but they looked, and were, as dangerous as death.

As I closed the door the sense of my peril almost overwhelmed me. The storm would surely break as soon as I was out of sight. I ran swiftly across the street into the protecting shadow and crouched down in a dark space between two houses. Cactus-like weeds were growing there and gave me a prickly time, but that was nothing to the sight of the soldiers pouring out of the shop like an angry and excited mob, buckling on belts, cartridge boxes and bayonets as they ran. Some had their muskets, others clearly were hurrying to get theirs, and all except two stragglers rushed out of the town in the direction from which I had entered.

I came out of my corner and hurried in the shadow down the road in the opposite direction to the one taken by the soldiers. Near the last house at the end of the street was a river; between the house and the water was an impenetrable barrier of giant cacti. I had either to swim the river or turn back, and it was just one imbecilic thought that caused me to turn back.

I reckoned that if I swam the river, which I could easily do, the cakes and bread I had bought would be soaked and probably ruined, and my hunger was so great that I just could not afford for that to happen. Besides which, I was quietly confident of my ability to beat my pursuers, who all seemed convinced that I had gone back along the road I had come by.

And so I retraced my steps. As I passed a house three

women came out. They spoke to me, and in my excitement instead of saying good evening to them in Spanish, I said good morning. That marked me down as a stranger.

At that moment four soldiers came hurrying down the street, and I made off to my former hiding-place. Then the three women did something which in my experience women seldom do: they betrayed the fugitive.

Calling to the soldiers, they pointed to my hiding-place. Suddenly all four of them were on top of me. I raised my revolver and snapped the trigger twice without result before they overpowered me.

There was a terrific hullabaloo as in response to their frenzied shouting their comrades came pouring down the street. They hustled me across the street into the shop, a mob that seemed like half a hundred, kicking and punching and yelling all at once. I was sure I was about to be lynched when the moment was saved by the appearance of their commander, a captain. Even he was no real saviour. He was a small, peppery young fellow, dictatorial and insulting, and clearly regarded me in my dishevelled state as a tramp and a rebel spy ripe for immediate execution.

It has always been my good luck to be able to suppress all fear when I've found myself in a desperate situation, so I now played the cold and haughty type. Flourishing my police passport, I told him I was Stanley W. Parish, of New York, a correspondent of the *New York Herald,* and he had better look to what he was about.

I hadn't reckoned on the fact, of course, that police passports made out in Havana had little currency in the face of the enemy, but mine at least proved that I hailed from Havana and not from a rebel camp, and as such it prevented the peppery captain from enjoying the pleasure of standing me up before his firing squad, which was the law for all captives in this savage civil war.

To make up for his evident disappointment, he sat,

pompous and important, on a barrel and ordered me to be roughly searched, and speedily there was a heap of gold and paper money on the barrel, surveyed by the captain with a covetous eye.

I had my $10,000 bonds pinned in the sleeve of my undershirt, which was the only thing they missed. What they found was my ring, five other valuable diamonds, my watch, which with its regular beat and stem-winding arrangement was a great curiosity, and my heap of money. The captain made great show of making out an inventory and statement while his party of half-breeds stood around, fingering everything on the barrel, a lodestone for all their hungry eyes.

My captors, so absorbed in the scene, had loosened their hold on me, and when their captain had the impertinence to put my watch in his pocket my patience snapped. I seized one of the revolvers, gave him a stinging blow with it, and sprang on him. We rolled, grappling, on the floor until I was dragged off by fifty hands. The captain picked himself up with blood running down his face. He rushed to a peg, seized a bayonet hanging there, and came at me like a mad bull. I jeered at him, calling him a coward and a freak, and undoubtedly that would have been the end of me had it not been for a woman in the shop who suddenly sprang forward and wrapped her arms around him, preventing him from lunging at me with the weapon.

And I can't say I was pleased he failed in his intention, for I preferred death to going back to Havana, the dreadful prospect of which was beginning to overwhelm me.

Ten days later, that prospect became a reality when I sailed into Havana a prisoner on board the gunboat *Santa Rita,* a wretched tub that steamed at four miles an hour and took more than a week to get from Puerto Nuevo to the capital. A guard of soldiers took me to the common prison, where an entire corridor was cleared of its inmates to make room for me and my guards.

My first night there was restless; when I finally woke and was breakfasting on some vile gruel I heard a cheerful voice greeting me in English, and I stiffened with involuntary displeasure. It was unforgettable, that voice.

"Good morning, Bidwell. I must say I'm happy to see you again. I must give you all the credit you deserve for your escape, but I should also say I haven't the slightest intention of letting you go again."

I turned and stood up from the table. It was of course Captain Curtin. He had one hand out to shake mine; under his other arm he had a box of cigars and a bottle of wine he had bought for me on his own account, and a letter from my wife.

My displeasure evaporating, I shook hands with this remarkable detective with all the warmth I could command.

14

REVENGE IS SWEET FOR THE
ENGLISH

How had he found me? How did he discover that the mysterious F. A. Warren, a man with no visible connections, was Austin Bidwell of New York? What were the clues that had led him step by step half-way across the world to find me living the life of a gentleman in Cuba, and causing me to become a fugitive in the jungle?

His story was not long telling. One of his men, named Perry, used to sleep in my little room with me, and every morning Curtin himself would relieve him, staying until dinner-time. We had many long talks on all sorts of subjects, and it didn't take him long to get round to the pursuit of F. A. Warren.

"My boss William Pinkerton started me off by telling me to try to find out Warren's identity," Curtin said. "Of course, I was only one of many who were put to work on your case.

"When I started I knew no more about you or the forgery than what I'd already read in the newspapers. I soon decided you were American, as had been suggested, and that you came either from New York or Chicago. That's because you were so young, and evidently had a good knowledge of finance and financial matters. And that led me first to Wall Street.

"I got a list of the names of every banker and broker in New York, and interviewed them all. With their help I made out a list of twenty possible Warrens, and gradually narrowed it down to four, one of whom was you.

"I found out where you lived, and began asking the neighbours questions. They thought you were in Europe, that you'd been there before, and that when you last returned you'd paid off debts and apparently had plenty of money. I became convinced you were Warren; my problem was to find out where you were.

"Some of your acquaintances had heard you say that whenever you struck it rich you would live in the tropics. That made me think of Florida.

"I went to Florida, and had a look round some of the resorts along the coast. At St. Augustine I sent letters to several of the West Indian islands, including Martinique, Jamaica and Cuba, asking for the names and descriptions of all wealthy young Americans who had arrived recently. One of these letters I sent to Dr. C. L. Houscomb, who was the best-known doctor in Havana, and in reply to my inquiry he gave me your name among others. The rest was easy."

(I should say in deference to Dr. Houscomb that after my arrest he wrote to tell me how grieved he was that he had betrayed me. He had thought Curtin was a reporter, and wanted the information simply as a matter of news.)

Ten days after my return to Havana in custody Curtin brought me a New York Herald containing these stories:

"Madrid, April 12, 1873.

"The American Ambassador, Gen. Sickles, has formally notified Senor Castelar that the American Government will consent to the surrender to the British Government of Austin Bidwell, now under arrest in Havana upon charge of being concerned in the Bank of England forgery."

"London, April 12, 1873.

"To the great gratification of the authorities here, official confirmation is given to the rumour that the Spanish Government has concluded to grant the extradition of Austin Bidwell, now under arrest in Havana. There seems no doubt that Bidwell is the mysterious Frederick Albert Warren, and there is very general curiosity to see him.

"Many conflicting stories have been published of his extra-ordinary escape and equally extraordinary capture. The Times' report had it that he was mortally wounded, and that he had on his person when captured diamonds to an enormous value, which had disappeared soon after. Sergeants Hayden and Green of the Bow Street force and Mr. Good of the Bank of England sail on the Java tomorrow to escort Bidwell to London."

Reading these reports, I was left in no doubt that the web was closing in on me. Even so I refused to give up. With the help of my friends outside, I made as hard a fight of it as I could to persuade the Captain-General to suspend the order for my delivery, and for a time I succeeded.

But after many delays and many plans, early one May morning I was taken down to the harbour. There the boat of the aptly named English warship *Vulture* was waiting, and I was formally transferred to the custody of the British Government. Perry, my prison guard, and the two sergeants, Hayden and Green, went on board with me. Soon afterwards she steamed out of the harbour. Later in the day the *Moselle,* the regular passenger steamer to Plymouth and Southampton, came out and about ten miles out at sea was met by the *Vulture's* boat, and I and my guardians were transferred to her.

I had at this point absolutely no intention of being taken back to England. The first night out of Havana I intended to jump overboard, wearing something to help keep me afloat. The waters of the Gulf were warm, there were many passing ships, and I would take my chance of surviving the night and being picked up. But Curtin must have guessed as much. With great cunning he not only brought my wife on board the *Moselle,* but allowed her to stay with me just like any other cabin passenger, shrewdly guessing that while she was there I would not do anything dangerous like going over the side on a chance.

Nunn was with us, too, feeling very badly over the

prospect of my future misery. He had held on to all the money I had given him, and I gave him more, for his constancy and affection.

We sailed into Plymouth on a June morning. I told my wife to go on to Southampton before I was taken ashore with my guardians. *The Times* of June 10, 1873, record-ed my arrival with due solemnity:

"Among the passengers who landed at Plymouth yes-terday morning from the royal mail steamer *Moselle* was Austin Bidwell, otherwise F. A. Warren, in charge of Detective Sergeants Michael Hayden and William Green, accompanied by Capt. John Curtin and Walter Perry of Mr. Pinkerton's staff. They were joined by Inspector Wallace and Detective Sergeant William Moss of the city police, who had come down from London the previous night to meet the steamer.

"It being known that Bidwell was expected from Havana in the *Moselle,* an enormous crowd assembled in Milbay Pier to await the return of the steam tender with the mail, in order to get a sight of the prisoner, and so great was the crowd that it was with some difficulty that Bidwell and his escort managed to reach cabs, and were driven to the Duke of Cornwall Hotel adjoining the rail-way station. They left by the 12.45 train for London. A crowd of 20,000 persons were present to see them off, and cheered Bidwell heartily.

"Bidwell will be taken before the Lord Mayor in the justice room at the Mansion House this morning."

The whole of London seemed to be on the move when I arrived with my escort. I should say that was none of my doing. It was apparently the day of the Derby. While that great Babylon was throbbing by the thousands to Epsom Downs, I, a poor weed drifting to rot on Lethe's wharf, was on my way to Newgate.

The sight of the grim granite fortress, a prison for 500 years, sent a cold shiver through me. Pacing its corridors on my first night's incarceration there, my mind dwelt on all the misery the place had witnessed. Next morning

I learned on the prison grapevine that Mac, George and Noyes were already there, but I wasn't allowed to see them.

In fact I wasn't allowed anything at all, despite that much-trumpeted aphorism of British justice that a man is innocent until proved guilty. The system of the convict prison was enforced here, and with the same iron rigour. The rule was strict silence, with no newspapers, no books, and no news at all from the outside world. This system was as cruel as it was unphilosophical, for while awaiting trial prisoners were left in an agony of mind which drove many of them insane or to the verge of insanity, the only way out when the past is remorse and the present and future are despair.

These were my thoughts while I was still presumed innocent in the eyes of the law; I was to have plenty of time later to come to terms with the reality that the system of British justice was and still is soaked in a desire for revenge.

There was for instance at that time no court of criminal appeal, as there was in America, so that when once the jury gives its verdict, that is the end of the matter. If a judge is prejudiced, or wants a man convicted, as was to be so in our case, he never escapes. The jury is always selected from the shopkeeping class, who are horribly subservient to the aristocratic classes. They don't care for evidence, they simply watch the judge. If he smiles, the prisoner may be innocent. If he frowns, then the prisoner is certainly guilty.

The system of legal representation through solicitors and barristers, so alien to an American, is an overt racket designed to enrich lawyers at the expense of natural justice. As no solicitor can plead in a higher court, so no Queen's Counsel will come in direct contact with a client, and must be "supported" by a barrister. So any unfortunate having a case in court must fee two, if not three, legal sharks to represent him, if represented at all.

Our solicitor was a Mr. David Howell, of 105

Cheapside, and a thoroughly unprincipled rogue he proved to be. He was a small, spare, undersized man, with little beady eyes, light complexion, red hair, and stubby beard, and he spoke with a thin, reedy voice. From first to last he managed our case in a way which would must have delighted the prosecution. He bled us at every opportunity, and altogether we paid him nearly $10,000. For this our defence by our eight lawyers – four Queen's Counsel and four barristers, only one of whom demonstrated enough ability to appear in an ordinary police court – was indescribably lame and idiotic. Howell, I am sure, had he been practising in America would have had to face a jury for robbing his clients.

Even today it is too painful for me to dwell for long on the incidents of our so-called trial, either the preliminary hearings before the Lord Mayor, Sir Sidney Waterlow, at the Mansion House, or at the High Court, to which we were committed. They certainly made big news in the newspapers, however, attracting attention all over the English-speaking world. The *Times* of London gave us this editorial in its issue of 13th August 1873:

"THE BANK FORGERIES

"Monday next has been fixed for the trial, and the depositions taken before the Lord Mayor at the Justice Room of the Mansion House by Mr. Oke, the chief clerk, have been printed for the convenience of the presiding judge and of the counsel on both sides. They extend over 242 folio pages, including the oral and documentary evidence, and make of themselves a thick volume, together with an elaborate index for ready reference. Within living memory there has been no such case for length and importance heard before any Lord Mayor of London in its preliminary stage, nor one which excited a greater amount of public interest from first to last. The Overend Gurney prosecution is the only one in late years which at all approaches it in those respects, but in that the printed depositions only extended over 164 folio pages, or much less than those in the Bank case, in which as many 108 witnesses gave evidence before the Lord Mayor, and the

preliminary examinations – twenty-three in number from first to last – lasted from the first of March until the 2d. of July, exclusive of the time spent in remands."

The session at the Old Bailey Central Criminal Court where we were to be tried had actually opened three days before that editorial was published, and the opening was reported by The Times like this:

"The court and streets were much crowded from the beginning, and continued so throughout the day. Alderman Sir Robert Carden, representing the Lord Mayor; Mr. Alderman Finis, Mr. Alderman Besley, Mr. Alderman Lawrence, M.P., Mr. Alderman Whetham and Mr. Alderman Ellis, as commissioners of the Court, occupied seats upon the bench, as did also Alderman Sheriff White.

"Sheriff Sir Frederick Perkins, Mr. Under-Sheriff Hewitt and Mr. Under-Sheriff Crosley, Mr. R. B. Green, Mr. R. W. Crawford, M.P., Governor of the Bank, Mr. Lyall, Deputy Governor, and Mr. Alfred de Rothschild were present. The members of the bar mustered in force, and the reserved seats were chiefly occupied by ladies. Mr. Hardinge Gifford, Q. C., (now Lord Chancellor of the British Empire), and Mr. Watkins Williams, Q. C., (instructed by Messrs Freshfield, the solicitors of the Bank) appeared as counsel for the prosecution."

Thus do the British cloak their retributive justice system with toytown titles which must sound very grand to them, but which are patently absurd to everyone else.

The one saving grace of our trial was that we were all in the dock together and therefore had for the first time since our last farewells the chance to exchange a few words. I was sorry to see that my companions were already much dejected by their fate, and no doubt by their experiences in Newgate. George was very cast down, and Noyes was in a state of perpetual gloom. Mac still had a glint in his eye, but he was a shadow of his old ebullient self. The British had ensured that their prisoners were nicely softened up for their final ordeal at the Old Bailey, which was to last for eight torturous days.

The misery and humiliation of those eight days! No words of mine can describe it, nor would I undergo it again for all the wealth of the world. We were pilloried in that horrible dock, a spectacle for the staring throngs that flocked to see the young Americans who had found a pregnable spot in the impregnable Bank of England.

Every day the court was filled with "fashionables", including ladies, who had come only to stare at misery. Outside, the corridors of the Old Bailey and the street were packed with thousands more, all apparently eager to catch a glimpse of us. Inside, the judge sat in a scarlet robe in solemn state, with members of the nobility or gouty aldermen in gold chains and robes on the bench beside him. The body of the court was filled with bewigged lawyers, a tippling lot of sharks and rogues. In the afternoon they were always half tipsy from their lunchtime punch or dry sherry, jesting and cracking jokes with each other and oblivious to the fate of their client paymasters.

In all there were more than 200 witnesses. About 50 of them were from America, come to trace our lives back through many previous years. As the forged bills were all sent by post, it was necessary to convict us by circumstantial evidence, which apart from the remarkable matter of the blotting paper seemed all exceedingly weak. But no matter what the evidence showed or did not show, everyone in court knew that our conviction was a foregone conclusion.

Late one evening the jury retired to consider their verdict and were back within a quarter of an hour, presumably having gone over all the evidence in that space of time, with their verdict of guilty against all four of us.

We had information that a few days before the verdict a meeting of judges had been held and our presiding judge, Mr. Justice Archibald, had been advised to pass a life sentence. Now, as the foreman of the jury sat down, the judge turned to the dock and began to address us with what we knew to be some truth:

"I have anxiously considered whether anything less than the maximum penalty of the law will be adequate to meet the requirements of this case, and I think not."

What he really meant to say was that he had anxiously considered whether anything less would be adequate to satisfy the Bank of England. Then he told us that we had not only inflicted great loss on the Bank, but had also seriously discredited that great institution in the eyes of the public.

"It is difficult to see the motives for this crime. It was not want, for you were in possession of a large sum of money. You are men of education, some of you speak the Continental languages, and you have travelled considerably. I see no reason to make any distinction between you, and let it be understood from the sentence which I am about to pass upon you that men of education" – and he might have added what he undoubtedly thought, Americans – "who commit crimes which none but men of education can commit must expect a terrible retribution, and that sentence is penal servitude for life. And I further order that each of you pay one-fourth of the costs of the prosecution, that is £49,000 each."

Threaded through this message of doom was indignation and a sense of outrage. Why? The answer was simply that we were young, American, and had successfully assaulted a British citadel, holding up to the laughter of the whole world its ostrich-like management, for had the Bank even so much as asked for such an ordinary thing as a reference we would never even have reached first base.

Anyone who does not think that our sentence for a crime against property was nothing short of barbaric need only contrast it with the sentence handed out in an English case of the same era. In that case the manager of a Warwickshire bank named Greenaway and three of the directors looted the bank for years by false balance sheets and perjured reports, finally robbing depositors of

£1 million. Several of the losers committed suicide, and thousands more were ruined.

Greenaway and his accomplices were tried, convicted, and being sentenced were told that because they were men of high social position, that disgrace in itself was severe punishment, and that fact would be taken into consideration. Two of the prisoners were then given eight months' jail, one got a year and the fourth got 14 months.

We were sentenced late at night – nearly 10 o'clock – a smoky, foggy London night. The court was packed, the corridors crowded; when the jury delivered their verdict the suppressed excitement exploded. But when the vindictive, savage sentence was pronounced an exclamation of horror passed through the crowded court.

We turned from the judge and went down the stairs to the entrance to the underground passage leading to Newgate. Then we halted briefly, each to shake hands and say our farewells. Ahead of us were the slow-moving days and the blackness and thick horror of the years to come, but we were comrades and friends still, and in that stone conduit we established a secret bond of sympathy in our separation, in the unlikely event that fortune might on some distant day turn her wheel and smile again.

"Never give up hope!" I hissed defiantly at the other three. "They will try to grind us to powder, but don't ever give up."

Mac, more workmanlike, said: "They always give you a Bible. Read a chapter every day, and while reading it think of the others."

It was a promise made and never broken.

I was marched back to my cell. The door was open and closed behind me, leaving me in pitch darkness.

Without bothering to undress, I groped my way to the little bed there and lay down on it. Through all that long and terrible night I lay passive, with a million dread images rushing through my mind. My eyes were wide open; I stared into the darkness, conscious that sanity and insanity were struggling for mastery within me while I, like some disinterested spectator, watched the struggle. Sometimes I felt as if I were struggling in the air with some powerful, unseen monster clutching my throat with an iron grip. A mighty space, an eternity of time, and daylight came.

Daylight – and nothing. I found a pin in my shirt and began to scratch a message on the wall. Even now I can remember what it was:

In the reproof of chance
Lies the true proof of men.

Then I thought of my friends and my promise. Sure enough, there was the Bible, an ill-smelling and dirty-looking one, on the dusty shelf. I read the first chapter at which the book opened, and concentrated my mind on my three friends. Then the book fell from my hands and my mind went into a whirling abyss.

I was sentenced on Wednesday. For three days, from Thursday to Sunday, my mind was a complete blank. I have no recollection of my removal under escort from Newgate to Pentonville.

On Sunday, day four of my sentence, like one rousing from a trance, I awoke to find myself shaven and shorn, dressed in a coarse convict uniform, in a rough cell of whitewashed brick. The small window had double bars over thick fluted glass which let in the light but prevented me from seeing anything outside. In the corner there was a rusty iron shelf. A board let into the brickwork served for bed, bench and table. A zinc jug and basin for water, with a wooden plate, spoon and salt dish (there was no knife and fork, nor would there ever be) completed the furnishings.

Even as I was looking round helplessly at these surroundings a key rattled in the lock and the door opened, admitting a uniformed warder. He gave me a searching look and said in a rough voice: "Come on, you'll do for chapel. You've put on the barmy long enough."

I followed him out of the door to the prison chapel.

No one else was there. I was told to sit on the front bench at the far end, in a division of the chapel which was separated from the main area of the building by a high partition. All the benches were simply flat boards ranged in rows. Presently the other prisoners came in, marching about two yards apart, and sat on the benches still with the same interval between them. A white-robed, surpliced clergyman took up a position in front of them and the service began, but I had no eye or ear, or any comprehension save in a dim manner, of what was going on. My mind was trying to connect the past and present, knowing that something terrible had happened to me but with no idea of what it was.

When the service was over I returned with the warder, who, when I came to my cell, ordered me to go in and close the door. I obeyed, banging it behind me. It had a spring lock, and when I heard the snap of the catch and looked at the narrow, barred window with its thick, fluted glass admitting only a dim light I remembered everything. It came upon me all at once then, the full horror of my position. I sat down on the little board fastened to the wall and buried my face in my hands.

Now I remembered too the promise I had made to my friends under the courtroom floor of the Old Bailey, and I resolved to live only in the future, never in the horrific present. As reason came back, so did resolution and courage.

I was in Pentonville Prison, in the suburbs of London, where all men convicted in England were sent for one year's solitary confinement. At the end of that first year they are drafted away to the public works' prisons, where, working in gangs, they complete their sentences.

There is nothing much anyone can say about the cruel torture of a year in solitary confinement. Suffice to say that I passed through a great deal of mental conflict, and at the end of it I believed I had grown stronger. I was eager to be transferred, with its prospect of looking at the sky and the faces of my fellow-men for at least a few hours a day

When at last that day came I was conducted under escort to Chatham Prison, 27 miles from London on the River Medway.

The first person I was taken to was the Governor, apparently an ex-army major and a pompous little fellow with a delicious swagger and an heroical air.

"You were sent here to work and you will have to do it or I will make you suffer for it," was his friendly greeting. To this he added a few more remarks of a very personal and pungent nature.

Next to the doctor, and after him the chaplain, who despite knowing who I was, asked me if I could read or write.

"Yes, sir," I replied meekly.

He offered me a book, saying: "Just pick a page and read it out loud to me." It occurred to me that he might be doubting my word.

Opening the book and pretending to read, I said in a solemn voice: "When time and place adhere, write me down an ass."

The chaplain took the book, looked at the open page, gazed solemnly at me and then wagged his head like a monkey, as much as to say, "You will come to no good."

A warder took me off and marched me down a narrow corridor packed on each side with what seemed to be little brick and stone boxes. Halting in front of one of them, he said: "This is your cell. You'll go out to labour in the morning."

Once more the key was turned on me, leaving me alone with my thoughts.

15

LIFE WITHOUT THE SLIGHTEST HOPE

I looked about my cell with a mixture of curiosity and consternation, for the thought had already struck me that this little box – eight feet six inches long, seven feet high, and five feet wide – could be my home for the rest of my life. On a small iron shelf I found a tin dish used by some previous occupant, smeared inside and out with gruel. There was no water in my jug, so when the prisoners were called in for dinner I approached one of the warders.

"Might I have some water to wash my dish?"

The fellow looked at me with undisguised contempt. "You're a precious one! Lick it off, man! You won't be wanting to waste gruel before long by washing your dish."

I looked around with interest at the other prisoners. They all had famished, wolfish looks; thin, gaunt and almost disguised out of all human resemblance by their ill-fitting, mud-covered garments and mud-splashed faces and hands. For some reason I was told to stay behind, so I watched them file out to their work, a ghastly march of spectres that haunted me for the rest of the day.

By nightfall, and suppertime, I had recovered my composure, and had determined myself never to look like any of the others. I finished the appalling meal cheerful and resolute to meet the worst and to take everything as it came. What came next after a night's comfortless sleep was breakfast of nine ounces of brown bread and one pint of gruel, and then the grim reality of "labour".

I was ordered to join 82 Party, a brickmaking party working in the "mud districts". Along with 1,200 other prisoners, I was marched out to work outside the prison grounds to a site that at once explained the mud-splashed appearance of the spectral array. There was mud everywhere, as far as the eye could see, and groups of weary men holding shovels or barrows, toiling away in it up to their knees.

A sort of road had been made across it with ashes and cinders, and our party of 22 men, with five other parties, moved steadily on for about a mile until we came to the clay banks, or pits. Here we were put in the charge of an officer named James. He wanted the work done and to achieve that used his tongue freely, but he treated his men as well as he dared under the brutal regime ruling in Chatham. He speedily ensured that I was given a barrow and spade.

A steam mill, or "pug", like a monster coffee mill, was used for mixing the clay and sand and delivering it in the form of bricks below, where another party received them and laid them out to dry, preparatory to firing them. Our duty was to keep the pug going, keep it full of clay to the top. The clay was in a high bank; we dug into it from the bottom and shovelled it as fast as possible into our barrows. In front of each man was a "run" formed by a line of planks eight inches wide and all converging forward and meeting near the pug. The distance we were wheeling was from thirty to forty yards, and the incline was really very steep, but the worst thing of it all was the sheer hard work of digging out the clay, and the fact that the pug had a gargantuan appetite.

There was no period of rest between the filling of the barrow and the start up the run. Within an hour my hands were covered with blood blisters and my left knee was giving me plenty of trouble from the slight wrench I gave it each time I struck in my spade with my left foot. I made no complaint, interested to see how the other prisoners fared. My curiosity was soon satisfied. About 10 o'clock the man next to me threw down his spade with an oath and swore he would do no more work. Putting on his jacket, he walked up to the warder and quite as a matter of course turned his back to him and put both hands behind him. The warder took out handcuffs and without any comment handcuffed his hands in that position.

"Stand with your back to the work," the warder commanded.

No one took the slightest notice, and the work didn't slacken for a moment. But one of our party was out of the game, and the rest of us had to make good his work.

Mid-day came. We dropped our spades, slipped on our jackets, and were quick-marched back to the prison. The handcuffed prisoner came trudging along behind us, and to my surprise I noticed that several of the other parties also had an enfant perdu, hands behind his back, marching in the rear. As soon as we were back at the prison each of these poor sheep in the rear fell out without even being ordered to do so. When all the men were inside a warder came up to the handcuffed ones.

"Right turn! Forward!" he shouted, and off went those poor fellows to the punishment cells for three days bread and water each, and no bed, unless you can call an oak plank a bed. What was so sad, I thought, was the matter-of-fact way in which everyone took it all.

The first day was over at last, but it seemed to me that something more had to come. That what I had gone through was just one day that would be like every other day for the rest of my life was surely impossible. Was there nothing ahead of me but isolation so complete that not a sound from the outside world could penetrate it, that world which compared with the death into which I was being absorbed seemed the only world of the living?

Had I nothing to anticipate but the most repulsive work under the most repulsive conditions? Wheeling mud for ever could not be the doom of any man; certainly it couldn't be mine. Inside my little cell was utter solitude; outside, the stillness of the grave. The ration which was my supper lay on the table, eight ounces of black bread. What was the point of cheating myself with hope? I was the victim of a vindictive sentence, literally barred from the world for the rest of my life. Yet I couldn't help but feel that that part of me which the bars couldn't hold, and which no man could deprive me of, was still my own, and that I would find support in it. So I resolved first to face the reality of the position, and second, not to cheat myself. Today I had seen the sort of men I was to live with. Now I determined to study and to understand the kind of life we were going to have to live together.

At early dawn we were called and received at once the nine ounces of bread and pint of oatmeal gruel which was our breakfast. At 6.30 we trudged to chapel to hear a schoolmaster drone through the morning prayers of the English Church service and listen to some hymn bawled out from throats with no understanding of tone or harmony. Then the morning hours would drag slowly by in the summer's sun or the winter's blast until midday, followed by the long march back to the prison for the midday meal, called dinner.

Each man went to his cell, where he was given his meal, sixteen ounces of boiled potatoes and five ounces of bread, varied on three days of the week with an additional five ounces of meat. At 1 p.m. the doors were unlocked and we were marched out to work again. At night, back at the prison, a further eight ounces of black bread were doled out for supper. Shut in between those narrow walls between supper and bedtime, one realised what it was to be a prisoner.

Soon after my arrival at Chatham I was placed in the same party as two Fenian prisoners, named Sergeant

McCarty and William O'Brien. It was strictly against the rules to talk, but the prisoners found ways round that, particularly if they did their work well. The officers were reported and fined if their men fell behind in their task, so if a man worked well he could break a rule or two; if he was backward the officer reported him for any infraction.

One day I gave O'Brien a hand fixing his run. We spoke, and soon became firm friends. He and McCarty were fine fellows and I developed a warm affection for them.

McCarty had been a sergeant in the British army for nearly 20 years. He had come out of the Indian mutiny with a splendid record and had been recommended for a commission. But while he was still in the army his heart warmed for Ireland and her cause. In 1867, when his battery was stationed in Dublin, he heard that the Fenians were going to try to seize the city with the idea of starting a revolt against British domination. With not much more thought, McCarty decided to throw in his lot with them; further, he got enough Irish soldier friends in his field battery to turn the guns on the British. The plan failed and McCarty, with many others, was arrested and tried for treason. He was sentenced to be hanged, but the sentence was later commuted to penal servitude for life.

O'Brien was an enthusiastic 17-year-old and an ardent Irish patriot. He had enlisted in a British regiment stationed in Ireland to familiarise himself with army procedure; to win recruits to the Fenian cause and, when the time came, to seize arms to start a revolt. The result of all this as far as my two friends were concerned was that they found themselves side by side in the great Chatham ship basin loading trucks with mud and clay, and all this on a diet of black bread and potatoes. The trucks each held four tons, there were three men to a truck, and the task was 19 trucks a day, and between the urging of officers, frightened themselves for fear the task might not be done, and the mud and hunger, it was despairing work.

The punishments were not only severe but liberally handed out. As a rule the men were willing to work, but between weakness, brought on by perpetual hunger, and the misery and incessant bullying of the officers, a few committed suicide each year. A few more deliberately maimed themselves; the favourite way was to thrust an arm or leg on the rails as a truck was being shifted and have it cut off. In 1874, the first year of my incarceration, 22 men did this. The object, of course, was to get out of the mud. A man with only one arm or leg couldn't handle a shovel and would be put in a cripples' party picking oakum or breaking stones. One of the advantages was that not working so hard he wouldn't feel so hungry. We were always on the verge of starvation, and in our hunger there was no vile refuse we would not devour if the chance presented itself.

O'Brien was a slight, delicate fellow, quite unfitted for the hardships and the toil of that place, but he was a high-spirited, brave youngster and his spirit carried him through, while many a man better fitted physically to survive gave in and died, or broke down and got sent away to an invalid station a human wreck. McCarty and I used to do extra work to shield O'Brien, and so long as our trucks were filled in time the officer made no complaint. The prisoners were certainly very good to each other, and usually did all they could to help and cheer up the weaker men.

In 1877 my two friends were liberated. I was glad for them, but I missed them sadly. McCarty, however, had suffered too much. He survived his freedom only a few days, dying in Dublin, to the grief of Irish patriots. O'Brien opened a tobacco shop in Dublin, where at the time of writing he still is.

I got to know all the Irish dynamiters – Daily, Dr. Gallagher, Eagan and others. They were paying dearly for their zeal in wanting to serve their country. The one

I pitied most was poor Gallagher. The strain on his spirit was too great; he soon broke down, and his dejected, forlorn looks, his stooping shoulders and listless walk made me think his days were numbered. He still lived some years later, when I last heard of him, but if he is to breathe the air a free man then his friends must agitate for his release, for he was then slowly sinking into his grave.

I had plenty of time to think about my working-party companions as I lay alone for hour after hour at the end of each day in my bleak, hard cell. I had plenty of time too to study the cell. In one corner was a board let into the stonework. In another corner there was a thin pallet and two blankets rolled up during the day that was supposed to be bedding. The pallet was so thin and hard that one might almost as well have slept on the board. For the first few weeks this bed made my bones ache. Most men have little patience and small fortitude, and this bed broke the hearts of many of the prisoners. And yet it was a trifle if only they had the wit to accept the thing philosophically and realise that they can soon become used to any hardship. It took six months for my bones to become accustomed to that hard bed, but after that I slept as sweetly upon that oak board as ever I did on a bed of down.

On a little rusty iron shelf, fixed in a corner, was our tinware, although it was actually zinc. The tinware was a jug for water, a bowl for washing and a pint dish for gruel, and the three pieces would respond to polishing. There were strict orders, rigidly enforced, that the tinware should be kept polished. The result of that was that the men never washed themselves and never took water in their jugs, for if they did their tinware would stain or "go off" as they called it, and then they would be reported and severely punished for having dirty tinware.

A prisoner was not permitted to receive anything from his friends or family or to communicate with them in any way, save only once in three months he was permitted to write and receive one letter, provided he was a good character and hadn't been reported for any infraction of the rules during the previous three months. If he had been reported the privilege of writing was postponed for three months, and as a result more than half the prisoners never had a chance to write during their imprisonment.

A visit of half an hour once in three months was permitted, but this was only granted on the same conditions as the privilege of letter-writing.

In due course I was to learn something of those who were to rule my life for so long.

The Board of Prison Commissioners have their headquarters at the Home Office in Parliament Street, London, and are under the control of the Home Secretary. One of these commissioners visits each convict prison every month to try any cases of insubordination which are too serious for the governor to decide, since he has authority only to order a few days' bread and water and loss of a limited number of remission marks.

There are four grades of prison warders – the chief warder, principal warders, warders and assistant warders. The chief warder is the most responsible of the prison officials, except perhaps for the medical officer, who is the autocrat of the place. If anything goes wrong it is the chief warder who gets all the blame; conversely, when things run smoothly, the governor gets all the thanks. The chief must be a bookkeeper, leader, disciplinarian, and responsible for all the day-to-day running of the prison. For these superior qualifications he is paid from £125 to £150 a year and his uniform.

In a large establishment there are a dozen or more principal warders, lieutenants of the Chief, and they have general supervision of the working parties. They earn about £100 a year plus uniform. Warders and assistant wards, who earn about £85 a year and £75 a year respectively, are provided with a short, heavy truncheon.

All promotions are by seniority. In case of transfer by authorities to any other prison they can retain their position in the line of promotion, but if they volunteer or make application to be transferred they have to begin at the bottom in reckoning the length of service for promotion.

Warders are exempt from doing night duty, which is all performed by assistant warders, who are on that shift one week in every three. I never saw one who did not detest it, because they have to remain on duty all night continuously for twelve hours, and are not allowed to read, sit down or lean against anything, or have their hands behind them.

Besides this, they often have to do a good deal of extra duty. They are allowed ten days' annual holiday but they usually have to take it piecemeal, a day or two at a time, so they can't go far away from the scene of their servitude. Any infringement of this military discipline, or rather despotism, is punished. Leaning against a wall or sitting down, for a first offence they are mulcted of anything from 3d. to 15d., and are put back in the line of promotion. I knew one officer, Joseph Matthews, who had been an assistant warder for twenty years because he was always being set back for doing some small favour to prisoners. He was eventually sacked, without a pension, for some slight breach of the regulations. He had a wife and six children and had worked twenty years for less than £1. 10s. a week.

Any warder who gives a convict a small bit of tobacco is heavily fined and suspended; if it is a second offence he is sacked without his pension. If he acts as go-between or facilitates correspondence with the friends or family of convicts he is sacked and possibly imprisoned. One assistant warder who was convicted of having received a bribe of £100 from a Newgate prisoner was imprisoned for 18 months. Another at Portsmouth got six months for sending and receiving letters for a prisoner, and such cases were very frequent.

The attitude of the warders and assistant warders is that they don't really care too much what the convicts do so long as they themselves don't get into trouble. So when they were not themselves under immediate surveillance the atmosphere relaxes. The warders are aware that the government grinds them down to 12 hours' daily duty on just enough pay to keep body and soul together; they are aware too that those higher up did far less work for much more money. "To be sure we can go out of the prison to sleep," they might say, "but otherwise we are bound as closely as the convicts are."

The trouble is that when a superior officer appears these same warders become as obsequious and fawning as whipped dogs, and recoup themselves for this forced humiliation by taking it out of any convict who makes any trouble. If the purpose of the present English system of penal servitude is to punish, then it surely over-reacts in that; if it is to reform, it fails hopelessly, for the moral qualities of most of the warders and their assistants are a barrier to any reformation; they are a class of men who by education and training possess none of the qualifications necessary for such a responsible position.

The business of the prison is carried on systematically by filling up forms, there are forms for everything. Every week a warder has to fill in a form certifying that every man in his ward has had a bath. I have known men to go unbathed for many months, for no other reason than that they didn't want a bath, and it saved the warder trouble (nearly everyone in the ward only bathed about once a month, anyway), and yet at the stated times the officer filled up and signed the form certifying that everyone had bathed at the regulation times.

Most of the officers are ex-soldiers and sailors who have been invalided out of the services or pensioned off after doing the twelve years for which they enlisted. In order to encourage enlistment into the army and navy, the government gives discharged soldiers and sailors preferential treatment in the civil service, and never mind their qualifications. So it is that you'll often find an assistant warder or a warder telling or exchanging obscene stories with prisoners, using the vilest language, and bandying thieves' slang. In my experience at least half of the officers I have known have morals on a level with the average prisoner. I did my best, therefore, to keep as great a distance from them as I could, and reserved my affections for those real prisoners' friends, the rats and mice which invaded my cell and which I tamed and taught to be my companions.

Not long after my arrival a prisoner gave me a young rat which cheered up an otherwise thoroughly miserable existence. The rat was a clean little fellow, passing all his time in preening his fur and scrupulously cleaning his hands and face. In due time I taught him to perform all sorts of tricks.

I made a small trapeze, with a pencil four inches long for the bar, which I wound with yarn and hung from strings, and the rat would perform on it like an acrobat, appearing to enjoy himself with his performance as much as he delighted me with it. I also made a long cord out of yarn, and he would climb up it like a sailor climbs up a rope. When the cord was stretched horizontally he would let his body sway under and travel along the cord, clinging by his hands and feet like a human performer.

A rat's natural position when eating a piece of bread is to sit on its haunches, but I trained this rat to stand upright on his feet, with his head up like a soldier. Placing him in front of me on the bed, I would hand him a piece of bread, which he would hold up to his mouth with his hands while standing erect. Keeping one sharp eye on me and the other on his food, the moment he noticed I wasn't looking he would gradually settle down on his haunches. When my eyes turned back to him he would instantly straighten himself up again, like a schoolboy caught out in some mischief.

My rat always showed intense jealousy of my tame mice, and I always had to take great care that he didn't get a chance to grab one. Once when I was training one of the mice I didn't notice that the rat was close by. Suddenly it leapt nearly two feet, seizing the mouse by the neck just as a tiger seizes its prey. I snatched it away at once, but I was too late; the rat's fierce bite had severed the mouse's jugular.

Like the rats, the mice were scrupulously clean and neat. Sometimes I had as many as half a dozen of them. I used to catch them by sticking a small bit of bread on the inside of my tin pint cup about half-way down; then, turning it bottom up on the floor, I raised one edge just high enough so that the mouse could enter, and let the edge of the cup rest on a splinter. It wouldn't be long before one would enter the cup. Once there he had to stand up, putting his hands on the side of the cup in order to get the bread, thus overbalancing the cup and causing it to drop, making him a prisoner.

I had one mouse which I taught to lie in the palm of my open hand with its four legs in the air, pretending to be dead, but with its little eyes wide open, fixed on my face. As soon as I said, "Come to life!" it would spring up, rush along my arm and disappear into my shirt like a flash.

I liked this fellow so much I was in constant fear a warder would see it and kill it. So in hope of getting a guarantee for his safety, one day when the medical officer on his round came to my cell with his retinue, I put my mouse through the "dead dog" performance. The little fellow lay in my hand with one of his twinkling eyes fixed on me, the other on these strangers. Such was his confidence in me that he went through the performance perfectly, and when I gave the signal he was into my shirt like a flash. The doctor laughed, and the retinue laughed too, of course. They all appeared so pleased that I felt certain they would order the warder (as was in their power) to let me keep my harmless pet, the companion of my solitude and misery.

They went outside the cell and lingered. After a

moment the warder came in, pulled the mouse out of my shirt, and put his heel on it. I am not ashamed to confess that I wept over the loss of this victim of over-confidence in the human race.

It was of course strictly against regulations for the convicts to keep rats and mice as pets, especially as the prison was overrun with them. But the warders had long since become weary of turning over the cells and prisoners daily, and knowing that convicts who lost their pets often reacted violently, there was generally a tacit understanding they wouldn't interfere, provided the pets were kept out of sight when the Governor made his rounds.

"Generally" was far from always, however. I once procured a beetle with red stripes across its wing sheaths and trained it to show some degree of intelligence. This was for months my only companion, but it was at last discovered by a warder and killed on the spot.

I made friends too with flies, and found they displayed considerable intelligence. I trained a dozen of them, and in the course of hours of observation I discovered that the males were quite tyrannical and did their best to keep the females away from getting any food. At daylight on a summer morning they would alight on the wall next to my bed and wait patiently until I put a little chewed bread on the back of my hand. Then there would be a rush, and the first male in possession would try to keep off all the others, chasing them away. This led to a succession of fierce encounters which were self-cancelling, since all the flies ended up by getting some food, and, I imagine, rather a lot of indigestion.

Sometimes I would allow a male fly to take possession of my forehead, and in the same way as with the bread he would then keep off intruders by darting at them in a ferocious manner, as if my forehead were his private domain.

Once I noticed a fly that had one of its hind legs turned up, apparently out of joint. As it was feeding on my hand, I tried to put my finger on the leg to press it down. I tried this three or four times and each time it moved away, but on subsequent attempts it seemed to recognise my kind intention and stood perfectly still while I pressed on the leg. I should say, though, that I failed to perform a successful surgical operation.

As winter approached the flies began to lose their legs and wings. Those that lost their wings first would walk along the wall until they came to the usual waiting spot, and as soon as I put a finger against the wall the maimed insect would crawl to the usual place on my hand for its breakfast. Such intimacy with despised creatures may make most people shudder, but the long years of solitude produced in me such an unutterable longing for the companionship of anything which had life that I never destroyed any kind of creature that found its way into my cell. Even when a mosquito landed on my face I would always let it have its fill undisturbed, and felt sufficiently repaid when it flew off with the music of its buzzing.

16

THE FOLK YOU FIND IN PRISON

In the cell next to mine was a prison genius with the Dickensian name of Heep, who was one of the most extraordinary men I ever met. He was born in Macclesfield of respectable tradespeople, as they are called in England. His father died when Heep was about five years old, and later his mother married a carpenter.

Young Heep couldn't remember a time since he could walk when he wasn't in some mischief. His stepfather was a severe parent, and thrashed him unmercifully for every bit of wrong. His mother didn't seem to think much of her new husband, judging from the fact that before the boy was 12 she told him to watch and follow his stepfather to the house of a woman whom she suspected was having an affair with him.

The boy had great natural gifts, and in good hands would have turned out something different from a lifelong prison drudge. He was handsome, genteel in appearance, and an apt scholar. His fault was that he was self-willed and headstrong, and as he grew up his naturally hot temper became uncontrollable.

At 15 he was so ungovernable that his stepfather had him put in the county lunatic asylum, where he stayed for 18 months before to the relief of the attendants he escaped and went to Liverpool. There he got a job in a shop dealing in bric-a-brac, rare books and antiques, showing so much integrity that he was often left in charge. Heep repaid that kindness by stealing a few items and selling them privately to the shop's customers. This went on until he stole a book and took it to a woman to whom he had previously sold several articles and offered it for a sovereign. Recognising it as an ancient illuminated Greek manuscript worth fifty times the price Heep was asking, she told him to come back for the money next evening. At the appointed time he arrived and was confronted by his master, who instead of turning him over to the police sacked him.

Heep's problem was drink, which turned him into a raving maniac. Not long after he was sacked from the antiques' shop, he was caught by the police acting in such a crazy way under the influence of drink that a magistrate had him sent to another lunatic asylum. There he apparently learned to develop his artistic skills, became a skilful copyist and landscape painter, while all the time planning to escape. That happened one night, when after going over the wall he broke into a tailor's shop to get some clothes to replace his asylum clothes, and set out across country. He had only gone about 20 miles when a policeman who had heard about the escape from the asylum arrested him on suspicion.

He was taken back to the asylum, and put on trial for stealing the tailor's clothes; for that he got five years penal servitude. When his term of imprisonment at Chatham was finished he was sent back under guard to the asylum.

Now it seems that according to English law if a lunatic in an asylum escapes and remains free for 14 days he can't be re-arrested and taken back unless he commits fresh acts of insanity. So Heep had to escape again, and succeeded after several futile attempts. He got work with a farmer, remaining safe for 13 days, and was congratulating himself that he would be free in one more day, when two attendants from the asylum arrived at the farm, seized him and took him back.

Poor Heep was now beside himself with desperation. He carried on in such a way that they shaved his head and blistered him as a punishment, and occasionally put him in a straitjacket. But he refused to be suppressed. On a raw November night, stark naked, head shaven, he went over the wall again and spent the rest of the night trying to sleep in a cemetery, where, miraculously, he found someone's old abandoned coat.

Next morning he exchanged the coat for a scarecrow's clothes, and walking on a few miles begged food at a labourer's cottage, and got a pair of old boots as well. As ragged, dilapidated vagabonds are common in England, no questions were asked and he went on, delighted with the freedom which he had been deprived of for ten years.

Heep got odd jobs at farms, bought some decent clothes, and eventually got work as a house-painter. While working at the house of a gentleman near Bradford he noticed a good many things that were surely worth money – no sooner thought than done, and that very same night, too! Unfortunately, however, he had a few drinks before turning burglar, and before he'd even left the house with his loot he fell into a drunkard's sleep still clutching the stolen goods. That's how the servants found him early next morning. They called the constable, and Heep got seven years for burglary.

His previous five-year stretch had given him some useful hints on how to survive prison life. The first thing he did was to pretend to go mad, persistently attempting suicide by cutting himself with glass. That got him permanently removed to the ward where they keep convict lunatics, and so he passed his seven years.

Discharged, he went to America and worked as a painter. Drink, and his vile temper in drink, soon cost him every job he took, and then stupidly he decided to return to England, the last place of all for any man who has once been a prisoner. Back in his own land, he squandered all his earnings, like a great majority of the working class in England, in the public house.

On a whim he decided to visit his home town of Macclesfield, arriving at the railway station an hour before the train was due to depart. To pass the hour away he went into the local public house and had several drinks. This so deranged him that on the train, convinced someone in the next carriage was going to murder him, he threw himself out of the window. Although the train was travelling at 40 miles an hour Heep wasn't seriously hurt, but there were enough witnesses to what happened to convince everyone he was mad, and he was taken off to the nearest lunatic asylum. It seems a tribute to Heep's intelligence that he behaved himself so impeccably among this new set of lunatics that the doctor discharged him as cured.

He got work painting some houses in Manchester, where there were some plumbers at work fitting gas pipes. In the street he met a young plumber who was out of work. The plumber told him he knew of a private job they might do together over the weekend if they had the tools for it; the proposal was that if Heep would leave the house on Saturday morning where he was painting and ask to borrow a few of the plumbers' tools for the weekend, the young man would share the payment with him. When the time came for Heep to borrow the tools he found the master plumber and his mate had already gone for the weekend, so he took the tools, which had been conveniently left in the house.

On Monday Heep started off to work early, so as to get the tools back before the other workmen arrived. Unfortunately, on the way he was stopped by a policeman, who asked him what he was carrying. Heep told him, showed him the key to the house where he was working, and asked the officer to accompany him there. Entering the house, Heep showed the policeman where he had been painting, and invited him to stay until the master plumber arrived. The policeman declined, and instead called another officer and arrested Heep.

When the master plumber arrived the two officers strongly induced him to make a charge against Heep for stealing tools worth ten shillings. The plumber, clearly under duress, at length agreed, whereupon Heep was so enraged that he seized the plumber's knife and cut his own throat, severing his windpipe. Three weeks later he was just well enough to appear before the magistrate, although he couldn't speak.

In those three weeks the police had found out all they wanted to know about Heep. They went to court armed with his criminal record, and recited it to the judge. Throughout his mock trial Heep was still unable to speak, and since at that time the Crown did not furnish a lawyer for the defence of those who couldn't afford to employ one, no one spoke for him.

"You are a man who has clearly found it easy to escape from ordinary asylums," intoned the judge. "So I intend to send you to a place where you will not be able to escape. You will go to prison, where you will serve penal servitude for ten years."

Although Heep was my nearest neighbour, it took many months of whispered conversations with him to extract his story. If I have dwelt too long on it, you must remember that locked in a tiny cell for the rest of my life, almost unable to communicate with any creatures but rats, mice, beetles and flies, I had ample time to reflect on this example of justice at work in the heart of the mighty British Empire.

Once convicted of a crime in England it is impossible for a man to obtain an honest livelihood, unless he has money, friends or a trade. All the large companies demand references that will cover a great part of the applicant's life, and strict inquiry is made to the last employer. Many unfortunates caught in this trap turn their eyes towards a new life in America. During my many years in Chatham I reckon probably five hundred convicts asked me for information about America, and at least 95 per cent were determined to go there when released.

A fair percentage of prisoners are men who have broken laws but are yet honourably minded and resolved in future to lead an honest life – these are not undesirable citizens. There is, however, another class, swarming in

English prisons, the professional criminals.

The conditions of society in England are such that the procession of these criminals, bred by the thousands in the slums and saloons of the great cities, is an unending one. The society that creates the criminal has also established a system of police repression that makes the life history of society's victims one of misery, until such time when the criminal, grown wise by experience, shakes the dust of England from his feet and transfers himself, a moral ruin, to America, where he becomes a curse and a burden.

The American Government has frequently protested to the British Government about this flow of moral sewage to her shores, but in vain. The officials in Britain indignantly deny that the State either encourages or assists the exodus of the criminal classes, but from my personal knowledge I know this is false. Let me explain why. In every English prison the walls are decorated with coloured posters issued by various help-the-prisoner societies appealing to the readers for patronage. "Join us", they all say; the message is that there is a life after prison, and often in the New World.

The lady who made "aid to prisoners" fashionable and a society fad in England is Elizabeth Fry. The English regard her as something of an icon; in fact she has much to answer for. Prisoners' Aid Societies have sprung up all over England, under the fostering care of the government, to the extent that all through his incarceration a prisoner is asking himself, "Which society shall I join?" He might opt for the largest, the Royal Prisoners' Aid Society of London, which has Her Majesty the Queen and a long list of lords and ladies for its "governors". What that quite means no one knows. Certainly no benefit from these people ever accrues to the discharged prisoners, but who can describe the glory that falls on the four or five reverend gentlemen, sons, nephews, or brothers of deans or bishops, who are the high-salaried secretaries of this particular society, and who pose at the annual meeting in Exeter Hall before a brilliant audience, just so that their names are reported in church and society journals?

The way the British Government accomplishes its task of unloading its criminal population on America and yet at the same time answers the charge of the American Government works like this.

Alone in the United Kingdom the Home Secretary possesses the power of pardoning. He directly controls every prison, his fiat being law in all things to every official as well as to every inmate. He has officially recognised and registered at the Home Office every prisoners' aid society in England, Scotland and Wales, and in order to boost them he gives every discharged prisoner an extra gratuity of £3 provided he "joins" a prisoners' aid society on his discharge, the result being that all do so.

England is a small, compact country, and the police have one head, the Home Secretary. Whenever a discharged prisoner is reconvicted for another crime he cannot escape recognition. In all such cases the Home Secretary notifies the particular aid society who received the prisoner on his discharge of the fact, very much to the annoyance of the society's officials, who are all anxious for a good record in reforming men who come officially under their auspices. They publish to the world that all who are never reported as reconvicted are reformed, and they need the number of reformed to be a big one to impress their subscribers at the all-important annual meeting. They achieve their number by counting all the ex-prisoners they hustle out of the country as reformed men.

Prisoners' aid societies are supported by subscriptions, which all go in salaries and office rents; the assistance given to the discharged prisoner is limited to the government's £3 extra gratuity. The London societies have an agreement with the Netherlands Line and the Wilson Line of steamers to "take to sea" for £2. 10s. all "working-men" they send to them. It is a simple dumping system, and a highly efficient one. I have spoken to many hundreds of men who joined one or other of these societies vowing they were going to America, and who were never heard of again in England. In the indirect way I have described, the British Government gave and continues to give to others all the help they needed. What the British Government subsequently told, and continues to tell the American Government at the time of writing, is a pack of lies.

One such society which is enjoying a boom is the Christian Aid Society, presided over by a Rev. Mr. Whitely. In 1892 Mr. Whitely told his annual meeting that 6,000 discharged prisoners had passed through the society's doors. By my calculation, 5,000 of them could now be in America.

Let me now take you through the procedure that ensnares a discharged prisoner. Two months before he is released he has to tell his warder which society he proposes to join. Let us say he chooses the Royal Society, another of its kind currently enjoying spectacular "success". The prison notifies the Home Office, which in turn notifies the society, and forwards a £3 warrant. Upon his discharge the prisoner takes a train to London and is met at the station on his arrival by an agent of the society, usually himself an ex-prisoner and always paid 21 shillings a week.

The agent pilots his man before the Reverend Secretary, and the dialogue is then as follows:

Secretary:	Well, my man, what do you intend to do?
Ex-prisoner:	I would like to go to America, sir.
Secretary:	Tut, tut, my man! You mean you want to go to sea.
Ex-prisoner: (taking the hint):	Yes, sir, I want to go to sea.
Secretary:	Very well, go with this agent, who will fix it with the ship's captain that you can go to sea.

If a steamer of either the Netherlands or the Wilson Lines is about to sail the ex-prisoner is taken on board in steerage. Just before sailing the agent hands him a ticket, and the former criminal is safely off to America. The Royal Society has one more "reformed" man to put in its report, and England is rid of a bad subject. If the prisoner had served more than five years, he may have a small bonus from the government in addition to his £3 gratuity; at any rate, the society is not a cent out of pocket over him and, forlorn and friendless, he lands in the United States with from $2 to $12 in his pocket. Almost certainly he will quickly drift into crime, spending the remainder of his life in either prison or the poorhouse.

All this, of course, could easily be stopped at the American end. An American tax of $40 on the steamship companies for every passenger not an American whom they bring to America couldn't be paid by more than one discharged criminal in a thousand. Or the American Government could ask the British Home Office for photographs, marks and measurements of all their discharged criminals, and send copies of them to all the immigration ports, where they could be rejected on arrival.

Very few English ex-criminals who get to America return home. I only ever met two or three, and sadly they were not only back in England but back in prison.

Six years after I was put in prison I was put in a party where I had a chance to learn bricklaying, and becoming something of an expert at it subsequently I was put in charge of all bricklaying. Eleven years after that, when I was the prison's oldest resident, and had some little influence in a quiet way, a man working in my party slipped a note into my hand that had been given him for me in chapel that morning. As in similar cases, I secreted the note and read it only when I was safe in my cell. The writer, whose name was Foster, said he was most anxious to have a chance to talk to me. He had been living in Chicago and could give me all the news. He ended by saying he was being murdered by hard work, and implored me to try to get him into my party, where things weren't quite so bad.

I was quite happy to do this, as in my party we were allowed to talk almost with impunity. To have a man near me fresh and only a year before in Chicago would be like a letter from home and also a newspaper. I was on the best of terms with our officer and when a day or two later one of our men was fortunate enough – in the Chatham view of it – to meet with an accident and be admitted to the infirmary I asked for Foster to replace him. With a trowel instead of a shovel now in his hand, Foster was delighted. We worked side by side, winter and summer, storm and shine, for two years, and I grew to like him very much. He was always truthful and fair-minded, qualities one may think incongruous in a professional burglar; nevertheless, he possessed them in plenty. But his four years' experience of Chicago undoubtedly increased his cunning without adding to his honesty.

Upon his release from his first term of imprisonment he joined the Christian Aid Society, from where Mr. Whitely, the secretary, promptly "sent him to sea". He arrived in Chicago penniless but within an hour met an old burglar friend who had been a prisoner with him in London, a man named Turtle, "sent to sea" by Mr. Whitely only two years previously. It was plain from Turtle's magnificent diamond pin and big bankroll, freely displayed, that the American way of life was proving attractive for this former protégé of the Christian Aid Society. He was delighted to meet Foster, and took him to a tailor's to be fitted out liberally, giving him $250 in addition just for pocket money.

Foster naturally thought that next day Turtle would give him his first burglary job to do, for where else would all these riches have come from? Turtle was aghast at the suggestion.

"I'm not a crook," he protested. "I'm an honest businessman – and it pays much better than burglary."

He took Foster to his city office, where he explained he had two city detectives as "sleeping partners", who turned over to him all sorts of villainous business in which there was a chance of mutual profit. And there was plenty, for Turtle had the ear of all the magistrates, and was in with all the gangs that made Chicago City Hall the biggest den of thieves on earth.

Turtle took Foster on his staff, so that with the two English thieves and the two American ones at Police Headquarters, they had a useful combination. As an example of the sort of things they would get up to, Foster told me the story of the Tennessee rancher.

The rancher appeared one day at Police Headquarters and told the two crooked detectives that he had just been robbed of $20,000. His coat pocket had been cut open, he explained, and the money taken while he was walking in a crowd. He produced the cut coat as evidence.

The two detectives thought about it. Why, they wondered, should a man be carrying $20,000 in his coat? And why had the pickpocket cut the pocket from inside the coat, when the natural way of entry would be to cut it from the outside, supposing he knew that the money was there in the first place? The more they thought about it, the more the two detectives figured there was a catch in the story, and the more they figured that, the more convinced they became that somewhere, somehow, there was something in it for them.

What they didn't know at this point was that the rancher had recently defrauded a Tennessee widow, who had opened a hotel after her husband was killed in the Confederate army, of the $20,000. This widow had wisely refused to take the rancher as her second husband, but had unwisely allowed him to become her financial adviser, and entrusted all her money to him. He told her he would go to Chicago to get it invested, but once there he robbed himself, sent the money back to his own address in Tennessee in a registered letter, and trotted into Police Headquarters with his implausible story.

The two detectives pretended to believe the rancher's story, but for fear that some of the other cops might hear and want a share they hurried him off to a safe house, while one of them went to Turtle's office and posted him in on the situation.

The rancher was anxious to leave town, but on various pretexts the detectives managed to hold him for two days. After that, they had to take some decisive measures to get to the truth and, they hoped, the money.

So far Turtle and Foster hadn't seen the rancher. The detectives asked the rancher to stay one more night in his hotel to see if they could catch the man who had robbed him. That afternoon one of Turtle's staff booked a room at the hotel and, slipping into the rancher's room, hid some burglary tools under his mattress.

A little while after that the detectives walked the rancher along Clark Street, and as they had arranged, Turtle and one of his staff met them. Turtle shook hands with the two detectives.

"Have you arrested this man for something?" Turtle inquired, jerking his thumb at the rancher.

"Good heavens, no!" replied one of the detectives, feigning shock and horror. "This is a wealthy Southern gentleman helping us with some inquiries."

Turtle laughed. "He's nothing of the sort!" he said. "I know him from years ago. He's a well-known Southern burglar. I bet you'll find evidence of what he's up to in Chicago somewhere in his hotel room. When you've looked, bring him down to my office and I'll show you his mug-shot in my files."

The detectives now addressed the rancher in a much more hostile fashion, and he, with his guilty conscience, got scared. They arrested him, took him to his hotel room, and found the burglary tools.

"You'll probably get ten years for this," one of the detectives told him.

The next stop was Turtle's office, where they strip-searched him. To their disappointment they found no money, but they did find a post-office receipt for a registered letter sent to Nashville. The rancher was held in custody for the night while Turtle took the first train for Nashville with the receipt in his pocket. The registered letter proved to be a bulky one, and tearing it open Turtle found the $20,000 in United States greenbacks. Next day all but $1,000, which was reserved for the victim, was divided among the four birds of prey.

They took the rancher before a friendly magistrate who committed him in custody to await trial. Twenty-four hours later one of Turtle's men called on him in jail and gave him the option of taking $1,000 and getting out of town by the first train or risking ten years for possessing burglary tools. With trembling eagerness he took the first option. Within an hour a bail bond was filled up and darkness found the baffled fellow speeding westwards, never again to return to Tennessee.

I am pleased to say that a long time afterwards I was able personally to discover that the story ended happily for the lady hotelier who was robbed. The catastrophe drove her back to her hotel again, where she prospered once more and then married a rich Southerner.

As for Foster, he spent four years in Chicago and flourished in his partnership with Turtle, robbing the city and citizens with impunity. Stupidly, he took it into his head one day to visit his old haunts in England, keen to display his diamonds and his bankroll to those of his former cronies who were still at liberty.

In London he played the role of a rich American but was recognised by the police. They raked up an old charge, arrested him, put him on trial, and he was sentenced to ten years. He is still in Chatham. My guess is he will be discharged a broken man at the end of his sentence, and then he will "go to sea" again under the auspices of a prisoners' aid society. Recovering, I dare say he will eventually become an alderman, one of the city fathers of Chicago, for in my experience many men more immoral and more dangerous than Foster write "Alderman" before their names.

17

AMERICANS TO THE RESCUE!

I have recounted how, the Sunday after my sentence, in my despair I took the little Bible off my shelf. The other books which in due time I had at Chatham were a dictionary and The Life of the Prophet Jeremiah. Once I took the Jeremiah down from the shelf but quickly put it back and swore never to take it down again, and I never did. A dictionary is a useful book, but it grows tiresome at times. As for the Bible, it was to last me for a long time. Every Sunday for 14 years, from mid-day until 2, I used to pace the stone floor of my cell preaching a sermon with no audience but my rat and my mice. My intention was to occupy my thoughts and to keep my mind bright, and I am sure it saved my life and reason.

Even so, after ten or 12 years I began to grow weary of the Bible, and longed for a Shakespeare. I was desperate for intellectual stimulation; never was a kingdom so cheerfully offered for a horse as I would have offered mine for an octavo. I had heard on the grapevine that my friends outside were campaigning for me, writing letters to the British Government, although with no success. They had interested the American ambassador in London in my case, and he had promised to write to the Home Secretary, but that was a year ago, and nothing had come of it.

Nothing – but not quite nothing. One evening, after another arduous day's toil, I returned to my cell hungry, cold, wet and miserable. There was a book lying on the board. I picked it up, spellbound, and read the title:

"The Complete Works of William Shakespeare."[1] No human being could ever have felt the kind of gratitude for another as I felt at that moment for the American ambassador. From that moment a new light streamed through the fluted glass of my window, and the world was a magnificent place to be in.

Then another piece of luck came my way. There was a smallpox scare outside the prison, and everyone inside had to be vaccinated. When the doctor came round a few days afterwards to examine the effects of the vaccination on me he found my arm so swollen that he ordered me to the prison hospital.

It was the first time I had ever been admitted, and the change from the horrible mud hole to the rest and comfort of a hospital cell was stunning. With nothing to do for 25 days but read my Shakespeare I was willing to believe that I was actually in the best place in the world. All this happiness was achieved by a single book, transforming gloom and misery into light. How many other convicts in that place, I wondered, had ever known such contentment.

Few if any was my own answer, for I had closely studied the effects of the unnatural life upon them. They arrived full of resolution, buoyed up by hopes they were soon to find illusory. The short-term men, those with seven or ten year sentences, could face the prospect reasonably hopefully. There was no such hope for the long-termers, those with 20 years or life, who watched a significant proportion of their own numbers taken to their graves.

The first part of their body to be visibly affected by the effects on them of hunger and torment of mind is the neck. The flesh shrinks, disappears, and leaves what look like two artificial props to support the head. As time goes on the erect posture grows bent; instead of standing up straight the knees bulge outward as though unable to support the body's weight, and the convict drags himself along in a kind of despondent shuffle.

Another year or two and his shoulders are bent forward. He carries his arms habitually before him now; he has grown moody, seldom speaks to anyone, or answers if spoken to.

His mind is keeping equal step with the general deterioration of his body, and so unfailing are the signs that even warders notice them, and remark to each other that so and so is "going off". When the sufferer begins to carry his arms in front of him, everyone understands that the end is coming. The projecting head, the sunken eye, the fixed, expressionless features are the outward exponents of the hopeless, sullen brooding within. And so he keeps on in that way, wasting more and more, body and soul, every day, until he drops, and is carried off to the infirmary to die.

An English prison is a vast machine in which a man counts for nothing. He is to the establishment what a bale of merchandise is to a merchant's warehouse. The prison doesn't look on him as a man at all; he is merely an object which must move in a certain rut and occupy a certain niche provided for it, and there is no room for the slightest sentiment.

Move with it, and all is well. Resist, and you will be crushed as inevitably as the man who ties himself to a railway when the train is coming. Without passion, without prejudice, but also without pity and without remorse, the machine crushes and passes on. The dead man is carried to his grave, and in ten minutes is as much forgotten as though he had never existed.

The plank bed, the solitary confinement, the bread-and-water diet, unauthorised but nonetheless effective clubbing at the hands of warders, the cold in the punishment cells penetrating to the very marrow of the bones, weakness, sickness and unpitied death are the certain fate of the rebel. Some are idiotic enough to invite it upon themselves, though fewer now than formerly. The progress of education, the philanthropic efforts of private persons, the "sending to sea", have all helped to thin the prison population. The judges too have been forced by public opinion to be less severe, although frequently nothing can be more capricious than the sentences they pass.

The law sets limits in very few cases. "Life or any term not less than five years" is the customary reading of the statute books, and the consequence is that one judge will give his man five years, while another will condemn his to twenty for precisely the same crime committed under precisely the same circumstances. I have too often seen a man who had been sentenced to five years for murder working alongside another whose sentence was twenty years for some crime against property. Such contrasts excite great discontent, and are sometimes the reason why convicts set up a hopeless resistance to what they feel to be persecution and injustice.

In the second half of the nineteenth century the British Board of Prison Directors got things altogether wrong, in my view. They appeared to think that in their dealings with convicts the only course was to apply "force, iron force", as one of the governors expressed it. Whatever they could think of to harden, degrade, insult, to inflict every form or suffering, physical and mental, which a man could undergo and still survive, was embodied in the rules they made. Their prisons were to be places of suffering and nothing but suffering. The majority of convicts in fact require no such brutal treatment, and the few difficult ones could easily be managed in another way. If prison discipline must be penal, it need not be ferocious and inhuman, as it certainly is in England.

Anyone who feels his sentence is unjust, and almost all feel that way, has as his last forlorn hope a petition to the Home Secretary. Prisoners, with nothing to think about but the day they may one day be released, set greater store by petitions than they can ever hope to achieve. They are the drowning man's straw, and as effective. First, they have to be written, and to some convicts reading and writing are insoluble mysteries. Many spend an incredible amount of painful toil and mental wrestling in preparing their petition. One such was a burglar and fellow-convict named Niblo Clark, who, despite being incurably ill in the prison hospital was something of a character. Niblo spent a year preparing his petition, bizarrely deciding that after he had written the preamble the best way to catch the recipient's attention was to break into verse.

I kept a copy of it, and while I won't reproduce all of it, I will repeat enough for anyone to be able to assess the depth of Niblo's poetic accomplishment. The petition had the usual cover prepared by the governor, in which Niblo's case was registered as number Y 19, and the information that the present age of the prisoner was 40, and the date of the petition 15 January 1890. It stated that Niblo Clark was sentenced to 15 years at the Old Bailey in 1880 for burglary, and in the column for "Remarks" it stated: "In Hospital. Troublesome."

It began with the traditional opening which all petitioners had to copy out as a preliminary to the servile, grovelling style they were advised to adopt:

"To the Right Honourable Henry Mathews, Her Majesty's Principal Secretary of State for the Home Department:

The Petition of Niblo Clark Sheweth..."

and what followed was all pure Niblo.

"... the Right Honourable Secretary the great benefit your humble petitioner would derive by a speedy removal from this damp and foggy inhospitable Climate to a milder one; the atmosphere here his thoroughly prejudicial to your petitioners health and causes me to be a great Sufferer i am Suffering from asthma accompanied with bad attacks of Chronic bronchitis and have been now 3 long years Confined to a bed of Sickness in a Sad and pitiable Condition and upon those Clear grounds and physical proofs your petitioner humbly prays that it may please the Right Honourable Secretary to order my removal to a warmer and milder Climate.

"necessity also compels me to complain of repeated acts of injustice and Cruelty committed again me, and which in some respects Might Justly undergo the imputation of ferocity there are numbers and frivolous and false charges conspired against me and every time I am discharged from here *[the prison hospital]* the Governor takes them Separate one each and trys to murder me: I have been No less than Six weeks at one time on bread and Water accompanied with a little penal Class and all the officers are incouraged to practise all kinds of barbarious maltreatment against me and other sick men – there is one officer here place here for the express purpose of tantelizing me and other his Name is Warder Newcombe this officer sir has barbariously struck and assaulted patients on there Sick bed and Several has complained of it to the Governor – But I am Sorry to say its greatly fostered and incouraged especially upon me it is quite useless to complain of anything to the Governor."

Here poor Niblo must have drawn breath and decided that he could better state his case in verse:

"Right Honourable Sir I humbly beg that you will listen to my woe

for what I suffer in Chatham prison the one half you do not Know

From repeated attacks of this frightful disease I am getting worse each day

So I humbly trust you will have me removed without the least delay.

In making my request in poetry Sir I hope you wont think I am Joking

for the greatest favour you can bestowe upon me is to Send me back to Woking

For in this damp and foggy Climate its impossible to ever get better

So I humbly trust in addition to this you will grant me a Special letter

Another little case I wish to State if you Sir will
Kindly listen

has it would Cause a Vast amount of talk all round
and about the prison

I mean if Niblo Clark should be sent upon some public Works

it would cause more talks than the late dispute
between the russians and the turks.

A regular marked man I have been for them all its
well known to Captain Harris

for the list of reports against me would reach from
this place to paris

So I humbly beg Right Honourable Sir you will grant
this humble petition

for I am sorry to State I have nothing to pay having
lost both health and remission

Such cruel injustice to poor Sick men is far from
being just and right

but to report Sick patients in hospital is the officers
Chief delight

But perhaps kind Sir you might imagine that they
only do this to a dodger

But its done to all – Austin Bidwell as well and like-
wise to poor Sir Roger *

like Savage lions in this infirmary the Officers about
are walking

to Catch and report a dying poor man for the frivolous Charge of talking

and when we go out from hospital our poor bodies
they try to Slaughter

by taking these reports one at the time and Killing us
on bread and water."

And so it went on, Niblo Clark's last desperate hope,
the last plea for his life, written in doggerel from his sick

---

* Arthur Orton, son of a Wapping butcher, who had impersonated Sir
Roger Tichborne in order to claim the dead baronet's title and inheritance. He
was sentenced to 14 years, served mostly at Chatham, in 1874, for perjury. He
was released on parole in 1884 and died in 1898.

bed to a stony-faced clerk in Whitehall, who doubtless sneered as he stamped it "No grounds" before confining it to a basement file. The petition was predictably rejected and Niblo died a slow, lingering death a year later, coughing blood on to his grey blankets (marked "H.M. Prison) from lungs weakened by cold and damp and the long bread-and-water regimes his desperation had brought upon him.

There was one petitioner, however, the only one I ever knew, who was successful, and I can record his triumph with enormous personal satisfaction. He was an enterprising young man named Frederick Barton, who arrived at Chatham with a ten-year sentence for forgery about five years after I went there. Barton was a fellow of impeccable manners and good appearance, and he soon became a favourite of everyone from the governor down.

Three years had gone by when one day he told me he was preparing a petition to the Home Secretary for a commutation of sentence. Much as I liked him, I had to tell him that I doubted very much if it would achieve anything. The petition was sent, and in a few days returned with the usual stamp: "No grounds."

Dejectedly, Barton showed me the paper.

"Perhaps you went about it the wrong way," I suggested, running my eye over the petition. "You should have made them think you had money. The English are educated with a lofty respect for the rights of property, you would have impressed them more if you'd said you were a millionaire."

"A millionaire? But I don't have sixpence. My old man is a private coachman in Tunbridge Wells."

An idea came suddenly to me.

"Let me try a petition for you," I said. "We'll try to get it sent in from the outside."

I had to convince him, because of his concern for my safety. I had a warder inside who for an occasional tip used to act as my postman, sending my letters to my friends and bringing in theirs to me. This of course was a deadly offence.

My warder friend duly supplied me with writing materials. I wrote one letter in my own handwriting and asked the warder to copy it. Both were addressed to Barton, and purported to come from two different relatives of his.

They informed him that his rich uncle had lately died and had left him $160,000 in cash and 16,000 acres of cotton land in India. It also said his father had gone to India to look after the property, and when he returned a petition would be sent to the Home Secretary, who it was hoped would grant his release. These two letters my warder friend sent to a friend of mine in London, with a note from me asking him to post them immediately.

I told Barton what I had done, at the same time telling him to say nothing to anyone. When in due course the letters arrived I instructed him to tell as many of the convicts and warders as possible, spreading the news across the prison.

We had in the prison at this time a wide-awake but tricky fellow named George Smith, who had been a clerk to a London firm of auctioneers and had been sentenced by probably the most savage judge on the bench, Commissioner Kerr, to 14 years for receiving a quantity of silverware, which he had his auctioneer employers sell for him. Smith was about to be released, so by my directions Barton made sure Smith knew of his good fortune, and that he had hoped on his father's return to be freed.

Smith, scenting the chance to make some money for himself, then did exactly what I expected him to do.

"There is no need to wait for your father's return, Barton," he said. "I'm going to be released in a few days and if you like I will send in a petition for you. It can't do you any harm and it may get you released immediately."

Barton at once accepted the offer, and told him that if the petition were successful he would give him the post of manager on the Indian estate, where he could start a new life. He also suggested that Smith should ask me to write the petition.

Smith managed to see me during the course of the day and thinking I knew nothing about the plot, explained it to me and asked me to write the petition. I promised to do so, and added that I would ensure it would be in London at some place where he could find it on the day of his discharge.

I wrote the petition in the usual obsequious style to the right honourable gentlemen in the Home Office, setting down all the wonderful good fortune that had befallen Barton *fils,* and sent it to Smith's London address.

Smith, like all prisoners about to be released, was transferred for his last few days to one of the thousand cells of Millbank Prison in the heart of London. On the morning of his discharge, and within an hour after passing through the gates of Millbank, he left the petition personally at the Home Office.

Two days later a clerk acknowledged its receipt with the gratifying assurance that it was under consideration. A week later Mr. Smith was notified that the release would be granted. He immediately telegraphed the news to my warder, who told me and I told Barton. Two days after that the release was received at Chatham, and Barton went wild with delight. So did all those who had heard of his supposed good fortune. Probably the only one who felt much disappointment was George Smith, who never heard of Barton again.

Of course, I was almost as delighted as Barton, although there was nothing in it for me beyond the satisfaction of seeing him freed, and the knowledge that after nearly 20 years in my stone cell, with the possibility of another 20 years there before I was carried out in my coffin, my wits hadn't entirely dried up. And indeed, they were soon to be exercised again.

A friend of mine had come over from America to see

me and to see if he could get any reduction in my sentence. My postman-warder was away at the moment, so letter-carrier facilities were cut off. I needed to communicate with my friend, and the only way was to apply to the Home Secretary explaining the position and asking him to let me write a letter immediately. At the end of eight weeks an answer came back that the Home Secretary had carefully considered the application and could find no sufficient grounds for advising Her Majesty to grant the prayer thereof.

The next day I obtained a petition sheet from the governor and wrote the following petition.

"To the Right Hon. Sir William V. Harcourt, Secretary of State for the Home Department:

"The petition of, etc., humbly showeth:

"That two months ago I petitioned the Home Secretary for permission to write two letters, explaining the urgency of the occasion and pointing out that the request was by no means unusual. Yesterday the answer arrived telling me, with as much truth, I have no doubt, as kindness, the anxiety with which the right honourable gentleman has been for eight weeks considering the petition.

"I hasten to express to the Home Secretary the regret I feel at the thought of causing him so much concern, to the inevitable great neglect of the public business, for as every prisoner knows there is not the slightest difficulty in sending out as many clandestine letters as he chooses.

"Now this being an infraction of the rules, any reasonable man would rather go along in a friendly spirit with the prison authorities than be at odds with them, but when trifling favours are thus refused, all authority is swept aside with contempt and the forbidden favour taken.

"I trust that this knowledge will save the Home Secretary any repetition of the anxiety he has suffered on this occasion, and while regretting want of success for myself, I desire to thank the right honourable gentleman for the kind attention he pays to my petitions for others.

"The Home Secretary will perhaps remember his merciful consideration of the case of Mr. Frederick Barton, whom he released some short time ago. It was I who invented Mr. Barton's fortune and wrote the petition which furnished the grounds for advising Her Most Gracious Majesty to extend her royal clemency to the deserving young man.

"The result of my petition did not surprise me, for I was always confident that an English gentleman could never be guilty of the solecism against English customs implied by keeping in prison a young gentleman who could be so fortunate as to fall heir to many bags of gold and 16,000 acres of cotton land in India.

"Mr. Barton had previously petitioned for mercy pointing out that he was only 17 at the time of his arrest, and asking that his extreme youth might plead for him. This petition the Home Secretary treated with very proper contempt, in delightful contrast to the respect and instant attention he showed to the petition of the young heir.

"You may imagine that it was with some comfort that I saw an English Home Secretary, with all the power of the Empire in his hands to protect him against imposition, releasing a criminal after reading a sheet of foolscap covered with lies, which had been left at the Home Office by a released convict. It is, however, the merest justice to add that Mr. Smith, who presented the petition, was as badly humbugged as the Home Secretary himself. The glitter of gold was flashed across his eyes as it was before the eyes of Sir William Harcourt, and with equal effect.

"But the slightest doubt never existed in my mind that the moment it became a question of money all distinctions would vanish and pickpocket and Home Secretary would scramble on to the same foothold.

"I beg to assure the Home Secretary that having every facility I need for sending letters as often as I please, I

shall never again cause him weeks of anxious consideration. Respectfully submitted.

AUSTIN BIDWELL."

Why, you may wonder? But why not? I had absolutely
nothing to lose, I was locked up for life, and in my stone
box I could still get some enjoyment from making the
pompous look stupid. I had hours of enjoyment imagining the look of purple rage on the face of some high-col-
lared clerk. And my goodness, I was living in a place
where a minute of enjoyment was at a premium.

The governor dared not violate the regulations by
refusing to forward the petition, which the regulations
also required him to read. He nonetheless sent for me in
hot haste and assumed a threatening air as I was
marched into his office.

"I am extremely upset, Bidwell," he stormed. "How
dare you play these kind of monkey tricks?"

I laughed. "Sir," I said, "this is a matter between me
and the Home Secretary. As I understand the rules, the
governor may not criticise or revise a petition, for in
doing so he would be usurping the powers of the Home
Secretary."

He puffed and blew and blustered, but saw I wouldn't
be intimidated. Actually, although he was a tough disciplinarian, he wasn't really a bad fellow.

"I don't want anything like this to occur again, or you
will be in most serious trouble," he said.

"You have my word for that, sir," I replied. In that
place of misery, I had had my little bit of fun.

Despite the antics of my fellow-prisoners as a source
of amusement, I was always saddened by the refinement
of cruelty which kept George, Mac and Noyes separated
from me in other prisons, and I longed for information
about them. After I had been in prison for ten years my
family felt that I and my comrades too had paid our due
to justice and ought to be liberated.

That year my sister came to England and remained
permanently there. She worked bravely and well on our

behalf, but with no success whatever, unprepared as she was for the vindictive fury of the Bank of England, whose powerful view would influence any government action.

But through my friendly warder acting as postman, and my sister, I heard what was happening to my friends and my brother. Fourteen years after our sentence, George, broken by the punitive prison life, was ill and bedridden and according to the prison medical officer would not live much longer. A month after this report I heard that he had been released to die. I also heard that Mac was in Dartmoor, and was bearing up, as was Noyes, who was in a prison in the west of England.

At Chatham, the evidence of what was likely to happen to me was clear to see. Out of more than 70 life prisoners none had lived to be liberated, and the Bank of England directors were clearly determined that I should not become the exception. But they reckoned without my brother George. Ill as he was, he rallied, and vowed he would not die until the three of us were liberated. From New York he set to work within the powers of his limited strength to campaign on our behalf. The U.S. President was told about his plight, and Secretary of State Blaine sent a strongly worded letter to the American ambassador in London, appealing for clemency. None of this achieved anything, but George refused to be discouraged. He wrote to the leading U.S. newspapers, who took up our case with enthusiasm. Unknown to me, people in London I had never seen, including Lady Henry Somerset and the Duke of Norfolk, championed our cause.

The years dragged on inexorably. When 1893 dawned I was in my twentieth year in prison. That winter was particularly cold, and I knew that the cold and damp were beginning to do for me, as they had done for most of the other lifers, and that the place I was confined to was the place where I would die. One frosty February night I was alone as usual in my stone cell. It was past 7 o'clock, and the prison gloom and stillness had settled down on all the inmates.

Suddenly there came the noise of hurrying footsteps echoing strangely from the arched roof as warders tramped loudly on the stone floor of the long corridor outside my cell. A rush of feet, or indeed anything that broke the horrible stillness at that hour, was startling. This I knew to be the reserve guard, which was never called out except when the patrol moving around the corridors in slippered feet discovered a suicide, a not infrequent happening.

I began to wonder who this heartbroken unfortunate who had ended his life of misery could be when to my horror I heard them advancing down my corridor. Outside my cell door they halted. I backed against the far wall in a frenzy of fear as I heard Ross, a principal officer whom I had known for 20 years, jangle his keys in the lock.

"Come out, Bidwell," Ross shouted, as the door swung open.

"What's the matter? What's happened?"

Ross grinned and pushed his face close to mine. "You're free," he said.

"No! I don't believe you."

"Come on, lad, it's all right," Ross said gently.

Like a man in a trance, I was led down the corridors into an office, where some papers were read to me. Other documents were given to me to sign, but for all the interest I could summon, all this might have been happening to the man in the moon. I was led out of the office, down some more corridors, and then I saw Ross thrust a key into the outer door. He turned, grinned again, and shook hands, and the door opened.

I looked up at the dark sky and saw a star, and then the beaming faces of friends were all around me.

APPENDIX

The trial of Austin and George Bidwell, George Macdonnell and Edwin Noyes.

What is noteworthy about the trial of the four Bank of England forgery conspirators was the zeal with which it was prosecuted.

The summoning of more than 100 witnesses, traced and brought to the Old Bailey within seven months of the fraud's discovery, testifies to the diligence with which the Bank's lawyers worked to bring the conspirators to book, and this after the incredible international police operation to track them down.

So overwhelming was the prosecution's evidence that when the trial opened on Monday 8th August, 1873, all four defence counsel pleaded urgently for more time to prepare their defence. The prosecution was to bring new evidence, it was suggested, some of which had been known about by the defence since only 10 days previously. They were to include witnesses who had not given evidence at the lower-court proceedings – the Lord Mayor's court at the Guildhall.

Mr. M'Intyre, QC. for Austin Bidwell, told the judge: "The prosecution should in fairness to the prisoners have given six weeks' notice of this new evidence and the prisoners are entitled, on every principle of justice, to an opportunity of defending themselves on the new points about to be raised."

Mr. Metcalf, QC. for George Macdonnell, said the

case for the prosecution had been doubled in extent since it left the Lord Mayor's court, that many new heads of evidence were about to be opened, and that it had been impossible in the nine or ten days since the notice had been served to make any inquiry about the statements the witnesses would be called upon to give.

The applications for more time were strongly opposed by one of the two QCs for the Crown, Mr. Hardinge Giffard. He said that although the case had lasted upwards of three months at the police court, the delay if any had arisen from the fact that Austin Bidwell had to be brought to England from Havana, and Macdonnell from New York. There was no legal obligation on the part of the prosecution to give the accused copies of fresh evidence, but such notice was invariably given out of mere fairness. Of the new witnesses, in fact, 40 were bank clerks and others who would if necessary give more formal proof on matters which had already been investigated.

The judge rejected the defence applications.

Mr. Giffard told the jury that the four men in the dock faced one count of uttering a forged bill but in fact there were 94 forged bills in all, and the effect of them was to obtain from the Bank of England a very considerable six-figure sum.

"You will therefore at once perceive that you are trying a charge of fraud for which you might seek in vain a parallel in the criminal annals of this country." he went on.

"And in the end you will probably have no doubt that the prisoners overcame all the very considerable difficulties they faced in order to bring about this fraud, and they did so with such consummate art that you may have a feeling of regret that they did not employ their talents to legitimate purposes in the ordinary business of life."

When the two Bidwells and Macdonnell came to England in the spring of the previous year they lived under various assumed names while they "set on foot an original scheme of fraud." The first difficulty they had to contend with was to secure an introduction to the Bank of England so that they might discount bills.

Mr. Giffard then told the jury of Austin Bidwell's encounter with "a respectable firm of tailors named Green in Savile Row," and how Mr. Green had obtained an introduction for Bidwell, whom he knew as F. A. Warren, at the Bank.

Bidwell told the Bank manager that he was an American contractor or agent charged with the introduction on an extensive scale of Pullman's sleeping cars into the U.K. and on the Continent, that he was about to build them in Birmingham and that he hoped to have some of them running in time for the impending exhibition in Vienna.

"Having obtained this all-important introduction to the Bank and having overcome all the preliminary difficulties, the next point with the persons concocting this gigantic fraud was to know what to forge.

"During September and October, therefore, they were actively engaged in various capitals and cities of Europe in making inquiries as to the solvency and status of the various large commercial houses, and the amount of respect their bills were likely to command in London, and in acquainting themselves generally with the ordinary course of trading transactions there and in this country, so that they might be perfectly armed at every step of the way."

Between November and January George Bidwell, under the name of Gilbert, procured a large number of bills, Mr. Giffard went on. These bills not only formed the model of the various forged ones, but being paid into the Bank of England and duly honoured, served to establish the mercantile credit of Warren there.

Bills to the amount of between £4,000 and £5,000 were obtained by the prisoners during those three months, their evident object being to get first-class paper and to induce the Bank to discount their bills.

"The prisoners next provided for the distribution of the plunder and their means of escape. It was manifestly impossible that the money could be withdrawn in gold alone and the prisoners no doubt felt that to receive it in banknotes was the most dangerous course they could adopt.

"This difficulty was surmounted by Austin Bidwell opening an account at the Continental Bank in Lombard Street, in the name of Charles Johnson Horton, into which he could pay the money received from the Bank of England and draw it out in a different shape."

Mr. Giffard then told the jury about the introduction into the scheme of Edwin Noyes. "He was set up for the part he had to play, and various precautions were taken to conceal his identity.

"Part of the plot was that Austin Bidwell, who had opened the account at the Bank of England, should be out of the country before the first forged bill was uttered. Noyes therefore acted as his messenger. But the other two prisoners, as to whom the Bank could have no information, were not only the persons who procured models for the forged bills, they also actually forged them.

"Suffice it to say that whenever the prisoners obtained a genuine bill they had the means in their hands to counterfeit it by having recourse to engravers."

Up to this time very good bills had been sent to the Bank for discount but before the forgeries began "a great coup was determined upon". Accordingly Austin Bidwell, early in January, obtained a large quantity of foreign money and left London for Paris.

"On his way there," continued Mr. Giffard, "he was considerably injured by an accident on the Great Northern Railway of France, but he turned this accident to account by introducing himself to Messrs Rothschild, who had a close financial connection with the railway company.

"He induced them, against their ordinary practice, to sell him a bill for £4,500* and with this he returned immediately to London.

"He had an interview with the Bank of England manager and complained in some degree that his bills were being unnecessarily watched, inasmuch as all which he had presented were of the highest possible character. He then threw down the bill of Messrs Rothschild, saying he supposed that that would be good enough for the Bank.

"It not being advisable for him to confess that he had left Birmingham and obtained the bill in Paris, he stated that the injuries from which he was suffering had been caused by a fall from his horse.

"He also stated that his workshops at Birmingham were full of new sleeping cars and he expected his transactions to be very large in the course of the ensuing month.

"The scheme involved not only the protection of the conspirators but also the safety of the plunder, and accordingly it was beyond all doubt that Austin Bidwell should be out of the country before the first forged bill reached the Bank of England.

"It was suggested at the preliminary examination before the Lord Mayor that because Austin Bidwell was out of the country he was not amenable for this offence. That was neither sound law nor common sense. There is a very old legal maxim that a man who did an act by another did it by himself. Bidwell might have done this at Rome or at Kamtschatka, but he would be equally responsible notwithstanding.

"On the 22nd January, 1873, in a letter signed by F. A. Warren, came the first batch of forged bills to the Bank. That was the first experiment, and if it passed muster the scheme was successful. If not, Austin Bidwell

---

* Austin Bidwell claims that the bill was for £6,000.

would then appear to have fled, and Noyes could set up the defence that he had merely acted as his clerk.

"The scheme was successful. Having got the first forged bill discounted the next step was to operate on the account previously opened, to get the plunder and to escape. But having obtained so much money, how were they to deal with it? Notes could be traced. The scheme contrived was as artful as the rest of the fraud.

"Anyone presenting banknotes at the Bank of England has a right to demand gold in exchange, but it might not be so generally known that the converse is equally the case, namely that a person tendering gold at the Bank can receive its equivalent in notes.

"The device adopted in this case was this. One of the prisoners went to the Bank with notes and obtained gold for them. Another of them went on the same day and obtained notes for the gold, so that unless it could be shown that the two prisoners were associated in a common design the connection between the fraud and the property actually obtained by it was broken.

"That process was repeated to such an extent that between the 21st January and 24th February very large amounts of money were changed, and immediately afterwards that money was spent on buying United States bonds.

"Austin Bidwell left London for Paris in mid-January and there married an English lady. He seems to have gone about France and Germany selling the bonds which had been bought in London and buying others with a view to destroying further all traces of the fraud."

The business up to this point was eminently successful, said Mr. Giffard. Every bill sent to the Bank was fabricated on the model of the genuine bills, Messrs Rothschild's included, which had previously been discounted.

The first forged bill would become due on 25th March, and it was so arranged that during the whole of the time the forged bills were pouring into the Bank

from Birmingham the genuine bills previously discounted were becoming due and being paid.

Mr. Giffard then told the jury how the forgery was
discovered "in a most accidental way" even while the
prisoners were making their plans to escape, by describing what happened when the Blydenstein bill was found
to be undated.

"What was Noyes' conduct when arrested?" Mr.
Giffard asked. "He knew that both Macdonnell and
George Bidwell were within the grasp of the law, but he
made no disclosure, and he merely gave an address at
Durrant's Hotel, where he had not slept for a fortnight.

"He thus gave his confederates time to collect the
plunder then lying at his and their lodgings, and to send
it to other countries, the result being that some part of it
remains unrecovered.

"A day or two later Macdonnell and George Bidwell
lit a large fire and destroyed all the plant used in the
course of this scheme. The same day they sent to New
York £45,000 worth of American bonds in a trunk
addressed to Major George Matthews, which has since
been seized by police."

The first prosecution witness was the Savile Row tailor Edward Hamilton Green, who was instrumental in
obtaining Austin Bidwell's Bank of England account.
When he took Bidwell to the Bank they were met by Mr.
Fenwick, the assistant manager.

"Mr. Fenwick asked Bidwell how he wanted to be
described, and he replied as an agent," said Mr. Green.

Mr. Green's son, Edward Green, said he had seen
Austin Bidwell more than 20 times at his father's place
of business.

Colonel Peregrine Madgwick Francis, the Bank of
England manger, said during "some conversations" with
Austin Bidwell the prisoner told him he had come over
to England "to introduce sundry inventions, first and
foremost among which were the sleeping cars.

"I asked him some particulars about an improved

brake but he excused himself from replying on the ground that it was a secret."

A number of letters from F. A. Warren to Colonel Francis were read out to the court. The manager said Bidwell had told him that in Birmingham he was staying with friends, and therefore all letters should be addressed to a P.O. box number.

He was asked in cross-examination: "Did you really discount bills amounting to these enormous sums for a man who had given as an address the post office in Birmingham?"

Colonel Francis replied: "That is so, but I had communicated with headquarters on the subject of the bills tendered for discount."

A procession of hotel staff, restaurant waiters, messengers, cabbies, and financiers and bank managers from all over the Continent followed him into the witness box to identify the four prisoners and thus piece together a blow-by-blow account of their daily activities across Europe in 1872-3.

There was little light relief in any of this evidence, but a reminder perhaps of the internal anxieties of big-time confidence tricksters, referred to by Austin Bidwell, when a Bank of England clerk described a visit made by George Macdonnell to the Bank's Weighing Room.

The clerk, H. W. Hughes, said Macdonnell, who had been to the Weighing Room on several previous occasions, arrived on 25th February (this was after Austin Bidwell had left England for good) with £1,000 in sovereigns which he wanted exchanged into notes.

"On this occasion the prisoner was kept waiting longer than usual and was very fidgety. He rang the bell once or twice and wanted to know the reason for the detention. He had been detained for half or three-quarters of an hour."

Some idea of the way Macdonnell and George Bidwell worked together on the fraud was given by Franz Herold, manager of the private hotel in St.

James's Place where Macdonnell stayed. The manager said a few days after his arrival at the hotel Macdonnell asked him to tell the servants when they came to his door to knock loudly and not to enter until he said "Come in."

Macdonnell also asked for large fires to be kept continually burning in his rooms, because, he said, he came from a hot climate in South America and felt very chilly.

George Bidwell called on Macdonnell nearly every day, sometimes as early as 7 a.m. He generally rang the front doorbell, and Macdonnell himself would go in his shirt-sleeves to open the door, as his rooms were near the entrance hall. George Bidwell would remain for most of the morning, coming in and going out regularly during that time.

The two men, said the manager, were always writing in the bedroom and used candles and gas almost day and night. They lighted all the gas burners there were in the rooms. The gas globes were all cracked from the pressure of the gas and the ceiling above the burners was very black.

The blinds were generally down in the daytime as well as at night. When the manager went into the room he used to notice papers, like bills of exchange, on the table.

Half a dozen engravers, die-inkers and stamp cutters testified to what George was doing when he came and went from Macdonnell's rooms during his morning visits. They spoke of George as being a regular caller, and detailed all the complex work they performed to order for him.

Typical of them was William Cheshire, who had a shop in Paternoster Row. George Bidwell was a frequent visitor there from December 1872 until February the following year.

In December George Bidwell gave an order for some lettering for the names of various Continental towns, and asked for them to be done in "fancy type". They included Amsterdam, Lübeck, Bremen, Hamburg and Berlin.

Mr. Cheshire prepared drawings which George Bidwell approved. When the blocks were ready Bidwell called, paid for them, and gave the name "Bohn". Mr. Cheshire did other work for Bidwell, and showed the court 25 impressions from the stamps he cut for him.

James Dalton, a deaf-mute engraver and woodcutter, who also had a shop in Paternoster Row, said George Bidwell gave him an order to print the words "London and Westminster Bank" and for some Dutch lettering. Later he had another order for the words "Hamburg Banking Co." and "Paid". Shown a forged bill by the prosecution, he said it had been printed from one of his blocks.

A handwriting expert, Charles Chabot, said the signature "Austin Bidwell" and bills endorsed with the signature "F. A. Warren" were in the same handwriting, as were the letters found in Macdonnell's luggage signed "Austin".

The defence called no witnesses, and the four accused did not give evidence on their own behalf.

Addressing the jury, Mr. M'Intyre, Austin Bidwell's counsel, made much of the fact that the Bank "had not sought fit to make any inquiries at the address which the prisoner gave in London, and although they had branches in Birmingham, they never instituted any investigation as to the solvency or the position of their customer".

It was "almost inconceivable" that the Bank should without suspicion have dealt so largely with a person who merely gave his address as the Post Office in Birmingham. In fact, the prosecution had failed to prove that Austin Bidwell was ever in Birmingham in his life.

It was quite clear that Austin Bidwell had money of his own, for before any of the forged bills were discounted £17,000 had passed through the Bank in respect of his account.

At one time, said Mr. M'Intyre, it might have been that Austin was willing to join the fraud "to some extent", but it was perfectly clear that after his accident on the French railway he changed his mind and had nothing further to do with the matter.

All the stamps and books were bought after he left, and not one of the forged bills was presented while he was in England.

Austin Bidwell's criticism during his narrative of counsel defending the accused might have appeared to have some justification when Mr. Metcalf, defending Macdonnell, told the court: "I have attended very carefully to the whole case on the part of my client, together with the summing up for the prosecution, and I do not think it would be attended with any good effect for me to address the jury."

Mr. Besley, QC, defending George Bidwell, made a similar statement. Mr. Besley was out of court at key points on several occasions during the trial, leaving George Bidwell to cross-examine witnesses on his own behalf from the dock.

George Macdonnell was then given permission to address the jury himself. It was an articulate statement, but long and rambling, and must have done no good to a cause already lost. He tried to suggest that Austin Bidwell was innocent, despite the judge telling him that he was not to address the jury on behalf of any other person than himself.

Austin Bidwell, he claimed, had changed his mind about participation in the fraud after his railway accident. "In those few moments of peril he made up his mind that he would have nothing to do with anything affecting his personal convenience, his liberty, his happiness in this world and his eternal happiness."

When Macdonnell began to talk about Noyes the judge stopped him, pointing out that Noyes was also defended by counsel, who would speak for him.

Noyes' counsel, Mr. Ribton QC, said Noyes' case was

entirely different from the other three; there was not a tittle of evidence to warrant the jury convicting him.

The principal plank in Noyes' defence arose from a strategy which Austin Bidwell does not mention in his narrative. In order to protect Noyes, the conspirators had told him on his arrival in England to put an advertisement in a newspaper applying for a situation as a clerk or partner.

There were a considerable number of replies, one of which was from Austin Bidwell, under the name of Horton. Noyes agreed to become "Horton's" clerk, and deposited with him £300 "as security", for which he was given a receipt. A formal agreement was then entered into between the parties, witnessed by a solicitor.

It was Noyes' case now that he had no reason to suspect that "Horton" was Bidwell, and simply carried out instructions he was given by his master. "Throughout the whole transaction he has been the innocent dupe of the other men," declared Mr. Ribton.

He told the jury: "With the exercise of courage, common sense, and intelligence, you will be able to discriminate between the cases of the prisoners, and to separate the innocent from the guilty."

Summing up, the judge told the jury they must not jump to the conclusion that because there had been concealment there had therefore been fraud. But on the other hand they must not be blind to the various clandestine steps which they would expect to find in cases of great fraud.

George Bidwell and Macdonnell, he said, had virtually admitted their guilt. Macdonnell had openly confessed his participation in the fraud, and George Bidwell had adopted his statement, although without that confession.

As far as Austin Bidwell was concerned, he had left England in January, yet if he had made arrangements for the forgery to be continued in his name he was just as guilty as if he had written and signed the bill himself.

After the jury had returned with their guilty verdict, the prisoners were asked if they had anything to say before sentence.

Austin Bidwell said he had nothing to say for himself, but he would take advantage of the only opportunity he would have to repair a wrong he had done to a gentleman then in court, and for which he was extremely sorry.

This was Colonel Francis, the Bank's manager, and he hoped that as the years rolled on the Colonel's resentment towards him would wear away. The manager had been the subject of much criticism, but any other man in his position would have been deceived in the same way.

"The only reparation I can make to him is to say how extremely and sincerely sorry I am to have deceived him in the manner in which I did."

Macdonnell said he had nothing to say for himself, but as far as the forgery was concerned Noyes knew nothing whatever about it, and had no idea of what was going to happen.

George Bidwell said he did not ask for any consideration for himself, but he asked that his brother, who was a young man and recently married, might be dealt with mercifully. He too claimed that Noyes had been kept in ignorance of the real state of affairs.

Noyes said the prosecution knew with what great reluctance he had come to London. He did not deny that he had already known the other prisoners, but when he arrived in London he knew nothing that was going to take place; it was not until later that he became aware anything was wrong.

The judge, passing sentence, described the fraud as a crime which, "for the audacity of its conception, the magnitude of the fraud perpetrated, and the misdirected skill and ingenuity with which it was attempted, is without parallel".

He could see no palliating or mitigating circumstances. "You were not pressed by want; on the contrary, you appear to have put into this nefarious scheme a considerable amount of money. How you became possessed of it does not appear.

"You were not ignorant or unable to contemplate the full effects of the crime you were committing. You were persons of education, so far, indeed, as I can apply that term to mere intellectual training, without any corresponding development of the moral sense.

"It is not the least atrocious part of your crime that you have given a severe blow to that business confidence which has been so long maintained and protected in this country. You, who now ask for mercy, and who are not restrained by law or honesty, must be met with a terrible retribution.

"If I could have conceived any case of forgery worse than this I should have endeavoured to take into consideration whether some punishment less than the maximum might be sufficient, but I cannot conceive a worse case, I cannot perceive any reason for mitigating the sentence."

EPILOGUE

Austin Bidwell was released in 1893 "with great reluctance" according to the Home Secretary, Henry Mathews, 20 years after he was sentenced, as a result of American pressure on the British government. He had been five years longer in prison than any Englishman had ever been kept on a forgery charge.

His English wife Jane divorced him soon after he was sentenced.

Bidwell was reunited with his family and his brother George in New York in March, 1893. The Bidwells at once set about campaigning for the release of their fellow conspirators, George Macdonnell ("Mac") and Edwin Noyes, claiming that it was unfair for two of the four, whom the sentencing judge had said should be treated equally, to remain in prison when two of them had been released. They visited Macdonnell's family, and a relative was sent to England with letters of introduction to the Duke of Norfolk and to the Roman Catholic Archbishop of Westminster.

The Duke of Norfolk in a personal interview with the Home Secretary said it was his opinion that the sentence was altogether too severe. This view, and those of other lobbyists, brought about the release of Macdonnell and Noyes.

They were each given steamer tickets to New York, and met each other for the first time in 20 years on Euston station in the summer of 1893. They embarked from Liverpool and were met at New York harbour by the Bidwell brothers, who immediately took them to dinner at the same Fifth Avenue hotel where Macdonnell and the Bidwells had dined the evening before their last voyage to Europe. Noyes afterwards said all four of them considered the dinner "miraculous", but in his view it was strangely muted.

There are conflicting stories of how much money the Bank of England actually lost. The Bank's view was that a considerable amount was never recovered, but there is no evidence that the conspirators lived lavishly after they were finally released.

George Bidwell had fulfilled his vow to see his friends liberated, and died shortly afterwards. Austin Bidwell turned his hand to publishing, but with limited success, and died almost penniless shortly after the end of the First World War. Neither Macdonnell nor Noyes were heard of again.

£10.000

London July 10th 1872

The Bank of England

Pay to ― Rudolph Kurzrull ―― or order

Ten Thousand Pounds ― sterling

F. A. Warren

A cheque for £10,000 signed by Austin Bidwell in his alias of "F.A. Warren".

239

LYMAN J. GAGE, President
HENRY R. SYMONDS, Vice-President
RICHARD J. STREET, Cashier
HOLMES HOGE, Assistant Cashier
FRANK E. BROWN, 2nd Asst. Cashier
Paid in Capital $3,000,000.
2670

First National Bank

Chicago, July 7 1893

Mr Austin Bidwell

Dear Sir.

I am glad to see you succeeding so well in your new start in life Your interesting if painful experience can be made valuable to others in a high degree I feel certain that in your efforts you will secure the respect and good will of those with whom you may come in contact

Yours truly

L J Gage

After his release from jail, Austin Bidwell received this letter from an American bank manager, complimenting him on his "new start in life" after his "interesting if painful experience."